HIDDEN TREASURES

BRISTOL VOL II

Edited by Simon Harwin

First published in Great Britain in 2002 by
YOUNG WRITERS
Remus House,
Coltsfoot Drive,
Peterborough, PE2 9JX
Telephone (01733) 890066

HB ISBN 0 75433 760 X
SB ISBN 0 75433 761 8

FOREWORD

This year, the Young Writers' Hidden Treasures competition proudly presents a showcase of the best poetic talent from over 72,000 up-and-coming writers nationwide.

Young Writers was established in 1991 and we are still successful, even in today's technologically-led world, in promoting and encouraging the reading and writing of poetry.

The thought, effort, imagination and hard work put into each poem impressed us all, and once again, the task of selecting poems was a difficult one, but nevertheless, an enjoyable experience.

We hope you are as pleased as we are with the final selection and that you and your family continue to be entertained with *Hidden Treasures Bristol Vol II* for many years to come.

CONTENTS

Courtney Primary School

Robert Fox	75
Kimberley Tsang	75
Billy Jukes	76
Lloyd Morgan	76
Chris Edis	77
Eddie Obree	77

Fromebank Junior School

Lisa Dark	78
Emma Hill	79
Kathryn Whiting	80
Benjamin Payne	80
Ellie Nichol	81
Amber L Ford	82
Gavin Pearce	82
Matthew Pearson	83
Sam Curry	84
Zoe Dunn	84

Henbury Court Primary School

Peter Kim	85
Kirk Wootten	86
Richard Still	86
Matthew Clements	87
Hannah Mossman	87
Lucy Martin	88
Fatjoni Skonja	88
Jake Still	89
Louise Banfield	89
Andrew Forde	90
Samantha Ford	90
George Bowerman	91
Jade Khan	92
Jamie Morris	92
Jessica Woods	93
Lacey McLeod	93
Corey Vigne	94
Shiny Kim	94

Kelly Ramage	95
Karl Edwards	95
Kimberley Porter Jones	96
Claire Meehan	96
Hannah Verdon	97
Alex Rolfe	97
Shannon Tingle	98
Sarah E Hollier	98
Tanya Hughes	99
Liam Wall	99
Gary Turner	100
Damien Elliott	100
Luke Mann & Matthew Hale	101
Sarah Gray	101
Shane Blake, Ryan Dowden,	
Carla Gilvear, Ben, Jodie, Rab & Michelle	102
Sammy Rees	102
Fraser Chandler-Jones	103
Jade Hancock	104
Emily Martin	104
Jo-Ann Scorrer	104
Michael Harris	105
Shane Mereweather	105

Holy Family School

Sarah Simmonds	106
Hannah Barry	106
Ross Williams	107
Andrew Collins	107
Charlotte Gaffey	108
Rebecca Arthur	108
Jessica Hogan	109
Jacob Scott	110
Tara Keary	111
Laura Bradford	112
Larry West	112
Daniel Roper	113
Sam Lawfull	113

The Poems

LITTLE MASTER MAX

Little Master Max
Decided to fax
His friend a newspaper letter.
He got into a fit
Because he couldn't do it
And decided he should do better.

He went to his father
Who said that he'd rather
Do something else instead.
He went to his mother
To find yet another
Place where he was led.

She told him to go
To a place where it snowed
To his uncle on Whitberry Street.
But when he got there
He was not there
So he sat down and got off his feet.

Little Master Max
Simply couldn't fax
His friend a newspaper letter.
He got into a fit
Because he couldn't do it
And decided he couldn't do better.

Sophie Kneller (10)
Colston's Girls' School

THE UNICORN

As I awake
The sun arises
And out of the window
In the cloudy sky,
I see the Unicorn of Dawn
With her long, white crystal hair
And her smooth soft skin as white as snow.
Her pointy curly horn shines like the morning star
And her light blue eyes sparkle in the distance.
It gets bright and brighter
As she moves closer and closer,
You can hear her neighing proudly
Spreading her peace.
As the sky grows lighter and lighter
I look up and see
The Unicorn of Dawn gone
So I crawl back into my warm, soft bed
And fall into a deep, deep sleep.

Rachel Jackson (11)
Colston's Girls' School

MISTY IN THE MIST

A sound from out of the mist, rings, rings
Tip-toe, tip-toe, quietly grumbles from the ground,
What is it? What is it?
The west wind whooshes the leaves as the
Mist slowly strolls away,
Leaving the noises fading, fading far away.

As the morning fights for light,
Another sound fills the air,
What is it? What is it?
The thing moves towards me,
Oh there you are Misty, you naughty dog!

Rachael Irving (10)
Colston's Girls' School

MY LITTLE HAMSTER

I have a little hamster,
He's small and weak.
He has beady little eyes and weeny feet.
So if you hear a noise at night,
It could be that cute little mite.
But this night I heard nothing at all
Nothing big and nothing small.
So I crept downstairs not daring to switch on the light
And then looked at him,
He seemed alright.
Then as I went nearer, just so I could see clearer,
Down my spine, I shivered with fear.
Then looked at him,
The poor little dear,
Lots of thoughts were running through my head and got stuck,

Is he dead?

Elizabeth Copeland (10)
Colston's Girls' School

MY DAY AT SCHOOL

At 8 o'clock I go to school,
I pass the dock and the swimming pool.
I meet my friend at the door
Which is by the school hall.
Also teachers are shouting,
'Hurry up kids! You are in school.'
We run quickly. We're out of breath.
Then my friend trips over her dress.
I pick her up to see if she's OK.
Then she says, 'Quick, let's hurry
If we want to be early.'
'But are you OK?'
'Yes, I'm fine! Now hurry up
Or we'll get a fine.
You know what Mr Mecham's like.
He'll shout at us till Christmas night!
Please don't let him give us a fright!
Dump your bags! Yes, we're in,
Hear that sound?'
                    Ring! Ring! Ring!

Alice Saunders (10)
Colston's Girls' School

SIZZLING SAUSAGES

Sizzling, sizzling sausages,
sizzling in a pan
going crack, pop, bang!
Sizzling, sizzling sausages
put them on a plate and gulp them down.

Lucy Mackenzie (10)
Colston's Girls' School

MY COLOURING BOOK

When I fill my colouring book,
how wonderful the pictures look!
I make things how I wish they were,
like leopards, all pink and lavender,
and red penguins, bright yellow goats,
and elephants with pea-green coats.
Light blue calves with rainbow noses,
black giraffes and gold, round roses.
Forests big with orange trees,
swarms with silver bumblebees,
zebras stripped with brown and red,
a bronze crow, a lilac head,
sheep brightly starred as the sky at night.
Everything's my special way,
colouring's fun on a rainy day.

Christiana Tziorta (11)
Colston's Girls' School

ELEPHANTS ARE RATHER BIG

Elephants are rather big,
Rather bigger than a twig,
Much bigger than a pig,
But . . .
Not as long as a train,
Not as long as an aeroplane,
Not as long as telephone lines,
Not as long as the Queen's
Dinner table where she dines,
But . . .
Elephants are rather big.

Ariana Ahmadi (11)
Colston's Girls' School

THE SNOW QUEEN

The night is black
but not alone,
the snow queen rises
from her throne.
Her mane is white
as white as snow,
her movement's quiet
and very slow.

Her skin is white
silk and smooth,
her hooves are golden
and magically move.
Her spiral horn
guides through the night.
The snow will fall
there is no light.

She runs so fast
and very smooth,
she jumps around
and hurts her hooves.
She stumbles back to her throne
and leaves the darkness all alone.

Hannah Ricketts (11)
Colston's Girls' School

MY DOG MURPHY

My dog Murphy is a black Labrador,
when I come home he runs to the door.
My dog Murphy likes a lot to eat;
his favourite dinner is gravy and meat.
My dog Murphy is eight years old;
he is very proud and very bold.

It makes him pleased and very happy
to be a dog owned by me.
My dog Murphy loves to paddle
or ride a horse without a saddle,
but what my dog Murphy likes most of all
is running and jumping and driving us up the wall!

Sophie Parkinson (10)
Colston's Girls' School

DREAMS

Dreams are good, dreams are bad, dreams are happy, dreams are sad.

Some people have dreams of their favourite foods like blueberry pie,
While you may have dreams of villains that die.
Exciting car chases explode in boys' minds,
While girls prefer dreaming of being Brad Pitt's brides.

Amazing dreams, annoying dreams, dazing dreams, brilliant dreams . . .
Cool dreams!

Some dreams make you mad, while others make you sad.
I like dreams that have a happy ending,
While you could have dreams of shopping and spending!
Any kind of dream that makes you smile,
Is definitely one that makes sleep worthwhile.

Smiley dreams, dreary dreams, cool dreams, absolutely fab dreams.
I love dreams.

Ellie Longhurst (11)
Colston's Girls' School

An Early Morning Start

The farmer comes out of the farmhouse,
Ready for the day to begin.
At three in the morning he starts to milk.
He gets the cows in for a bit of hard work.
He calls their names, Betty, Freda and Grace.
'Come on' he calls 'you are a disgrace.'
200 cows is the job in hand
And to be finished before 8 o'clock comes around.
Then it's time for the milk tanker, red and bright,
To take the milk, day and night.
Breakfast calls!
The job is done. Sizzling bacon, egg sunny side up,
And a cup of the white stuff to finish it up!

Chloe Green (10)
Colston's Girls' School

Penguin Small

Penguin small
grew very tall,
very tall grew he.

He made a splash
which sounded like a crash
then ran away in a flash.

Next job, to the Pole,
to dig a hole,
as fast as could be.

Oh no!

That's too deep, that's the end of me!

Eva Shearman (10)
Colston's Girls' School

THE JUNGLE

Noises in the jungle
Crickets singing loud
See the waterfall gleaming
crashing to the ground
Spy the apes swinging
from branch to branch
It's nothing like mountains
you can't get an avalanche
You can hear the snakes hissing,
slithering on the ground
if you listen carefully
you'll hear the beautiful sound,
the sound, the sound, the sound,

you'll hear the beautiful sound!

Jade Bryer (11)
Colston's Girls' School

THE STREAM POEM

The stream slithers down the mountainside
Like a scaly snake;
It tumbles down hills
Like a fall of rocks;
The stream splashes around the valleys
Like jumping fish,
And as it goes, it flows gently along
Like a rhyming verse.
Then, smoothly and neatly,
Its journey complete,
It comes to rest in a wide shining lake
And the poem is complete.

Kalila Sangster (10)
Colston's Girls' School

THE WRITER OF THIS POEM

The writer of this poem is bright as a button,
As beautiful as a butterfly.

The writer of this poem is as soft as a feather,
As warm as the summer's weather.

The writer of this poem is as courageous as a lion,
As colourful as a chameleon.

The writer of this poem is as precious as a ruby,
As rosy as a rose.

The writer of this poem is as gentle as the morning breeze,
As cuddly as a kitten.

The writer of this poem is as clever as a monkey,
As smart as can be - *just like me!*

Sunia Malik (10)
Colston's Girls' School

THE UNICORN

The unicorn galloped and galloped through the wood
The wonderful wood with the blazing blossom,
Amazing blazing blossom that shimmered with magic,
With the magic of the twisted unicorn's horn.
Her twisted horn sparkled in the glistening lake,
And the glistening lake enchanted the sunset.
Enchanted, the sunset filled the wood,
That wonderful wood with spectacular colours,
And spectacular colours shone
In the unicorn's horn,
The wondrous unicorn's horn.

Agnes Davidson (10)
Colston's Girls' School

THE RIVER

The winter river freezes
There are icicles hanging down.
The winter winds and chilly breezes
Make an eerie sound

The summer river's slow
Through hot and lazy days.
The water level's low
Where the children happily play

The autumn river floods
There are leaves along the ground.
Banks have turned to mud
And the leaves are shades of brown.

Elizabeth Morgan (11)
Colston's Girls' School

THE GLAD GAME!

Have you played the Glad Game?
When you're feeling full of gloom
You can't have what you want
And you only think of Doom?

That's when you must remember
Those things that happened right
Not what might have been.
Only move on
Trust me
All will become
b r i g h t!

Polly-RuAnna Martin (11)
Colston's Girls' School

COLOURS

Purple is the colour of violets
Blue is the colour of the sky
Brown is the colour of leaves.

Green is the colour of fresh grass
Orange is the colour of an orange.
Gold is the colour of golden coins
Silver is the colour of silver coins
Pink is the colour of a baby pig
Bronze is the colour of a pin.

Black is the colour of a black sheep.

But of all the colours I have here,
purple is the one I hold dear.

Siân Basham (10)
Colston's Girls' School

BLUE

A deep, dark blue sea,
Mammals like dolphins
Curve over a wave.

Camilla Sidgwick (11)
Colston's Girls' School

MUSIC LESSONS

We have music lessons twice a week,
When we go up the stairs they make a creak.
When we get in, we sit down,
The teacher comes in without a frown.
The lesson starts with a discussion,
Then sometimes we do percussion.
The keyboard can go high or low,
That's not all we know.
We sometimes come in late,
But the lesson still is great.
Music lessons are not very long,
Shame we can't play the gong.
Sometimes we sing,
Other times we make bells ring,
But soon it's time to go,
And walk across the playground below.

Mark Roberts (10)
Colston's Lower School

THE CHEETAH

The cheetah.
The fastest animal in the world.
Quick, sleek, wild.
Like a speeding bullet.
As quick as Concorde.
It makes me feel happy.
It reminds us of how we are not important.

Jonathan Cooke (10)
Colston's Lower School

MUSIC LESSON

The room is silent as we walk in,
as if it is waiting for us to begin.

Josh bangs on the drum,
while David tries to hum.
The clattering of the bells,*
sends shock waves round the cells.

Shivanni stands and sings a song,
but oh my goodness, the rhythm is wrong.
Ben and Amelia attempt to join in,
but create such a terrible din.

The teacher's hands are over his ears,
He cannot bear to sit and hear.
'Quiet class,' he stands and glares,
but does he realise this statement wears?

He gracefully plays a piece on the keyboard,
We stand to sing 'My Sweet Lord'.
Some sound flat, some sound sharp,
We do not sound like a flowing harp.

The bell rings, we jump up high,
As we leave, the room seems to let out a sigh.

Marcella Pinto (11)
Colston's Lower School

WINTER

Spider webs are hung with sparkling diamonds
and blanks of white snow-down litter the floor.
The tiny robin twitters away in the corner,
as winter falls over the country once more.

Ice covers every drop of water,
dull crackling brown leaves trapped underneath.
Naked branches spindly around us.
Waiting, just waiting, waiting for relief!

Grace Eccleson (10)
Colston's Lower School

OUR CHRISTMAS CONCERT

The Twelve Days of Christmas was our song,
We practised the actions whilst we sang along.
Would we remember all we were told,
At the same time as acting bold!
Concert time, showing nervous faces,
Hearts beat, reaching magnificent paces.
Sir is hoping we will sing,
And not be distracted by the rings.
Ben rushes out in his tree,
Standing there for all to see.
Mark is on, flapping wings,
Acting a dove, while the audience sings.
Max is here, looking queer,
Turning up his speed a gear.
If I went on in this way,
I'd probably be here all day!
But I must tell you of the way,
That Andrew Hinton danced that day!
The end in sight, we gave a bow,
And sighed a great big 'Wow!'
We finally finished, we'd had some fun,
And our bit was now over and done.

Joshua Krysiak (11)
Colston's Lower School

GHOSTS

With Sarah having such good ears,
Hears something weird.
They're all asleep, her family,
Well maybe.
Max awoke with a stutter,
To hear someone mutter.
It was Sarah,
Terror filled her little body.
She held tight her toy Noddy,
She said she heard talking,
And even them walking.
They crept down the creeping steps,
To only find a ghost that said,
'You should never, ever leave your bed,
The night belongs to the undead!
You shouldn't be here, we're free here
We will stay,
You can't keep us away.'

Laura Pugh (11)
Colston's Lower School

BLUE WHALE

The blue whale,
Soars through the sea,
Serene, strong, muscular,
Like a gentle giant,
Like a large building.
It makes me feel like a bean.
The blue whale,
Reminds us how small we are as human beings.

Jay Drew (11)
Colston's Lower School

MUSIC

We have music twice a week.
On Monday,
With Mr Holmes.
And,
On Wednesday.
With Mr Everington.

This term:
On Monday.
We are doing musical advertising,
On the keyboards with Mr Holmes.
On Wednesday
We do lots of singing
With Mr Everington.

Some people play instruments,
Like pianos and violins.
And, we have a mini-concert
Almost every week!

Ben Krawiec (11)
Colston's Lower School

THE COLD DAY

I went on my skis
And landed on my knees.
I was in for a freeze
And the cold made me sneeze.
I got out of that
Wearing gloves and a hat,
And went home to have a think
Whilst warming up with a drink.

Andrew Hinton (11)
Colston's Lower School

HAUNTED HOUSE

I stepped into a house,
Was it haunted? I do not know.
The floorboards creaked as I took my steps,
The rest was as quiet as a mouse.

I stepped into the hall,
With cautious steps.
The wind whistled against the dark and dirty windows,
The rest was as quiet as a closed mall.

I stepped into the living room,
Wondering if surprises lay ahead.
The brush of my foot swept dirt across the rug,
The rest was as quiet as a pharaoh's tomb.

I stepped into the kitchen,
With my mind on traps.
Rusty pots and pans clattered faintly against the wall,
The rest was as quiet as a spider twitchin'.

I stepped into the dining room,
But very shakily.
When I sat on the chairs they squeaked and creaked,
The rest was as quiet as a baby in the mother's womb.

I stepped into the cellar,
As frightened as ever.
The wind blowing through the cobwebs sounded like
opening an umbrella.
The rest was as quiet as a sleeping fella.

I stepped into the garden,
Relieved, like never before.
I pleasured at the wind blowing in my face,
The rest was as quiet as a Trappist Monk's pardon.

Ross Martinovic (10)
Colston's Lower School

18

THE HIGHWAYMAN

On the road from Bristol to London,
Rides the ghost of the old highwayman.
Many a carriage he robbed
Taking jewels from lady and man.

Till one day they vowed to stop him
To capture and make him despair
No more would he go a-robbing
After death in the village square.

So one frosty night he was ambushed
While riding back with a grin.
A band of lawmen caught him
And then they *'done him in!'*

On a Sunday morning soon after
The body was put in the stocks
But when the crowd came at lunchtime
They saw nothing but empty locks!

But now legend has it
On a cold frosty night
The drivers on the motorway
Will often get a fright.

For lit up in their headlights
Just a few yards ahead
Is the spectre of our highwayman
Is he really dead?

The reason his death's the question,
'Is he really dead?'
Is it's not his horse he's riding
But a two-fifty cc moped.

David Stone (10)
Colston's Lower School

THE PERFECT MUSIC LESSON

The perfect music lesson would be,
If we could play and chat, including me,
We could be on the keyboards, every lesson,
Certainly we would enjoy such lively sessions.

It would be brilliant we wouldn't ever have to sing,
We'd talk away until the bell would ring.
There would be no more awful concerts or choirs,
To our elders this might be quite dire.

We'd have this really groovy teacher,
A really wicked kind of creature,
He'd take the lessons, just how we told him,
He would listen to our every whim.

He'd let us take the headphones out,
So then we wouldn't sit and pout.
We'd dance and clap and sing and shout,
Until the time came when we'd rush out.

Amelia Beaton (10)
Colston's Lower School

THE MIGHTY TIGER

The mighty tiger
Been on land for hundreds of years.
Prowling, stealthily, hungry.
Like an orange quilt hiding in the grass.
The colour is like a fire on bonfire night.
It makes me feel weak and jealous.
It makes me feel like an antelope.
The mighty tiger
Reminds us how insignificant we are.

Otis Smart (10)
Colston's Lower School

THE FURNITURE GAME

She would be a soft bouncy sofa,
She would be noon.
She would be a beautiful, peaceful violin,
She would be a sticky sweet.
She would be a clean planet,
She would be a quiet song by S Club 7,
She would be an active game of netball,
She would be a beautiful, glistening swan.
She would be a cuddly, warm fleece,
She would be a trip to Florida,
She would be a quiet scooter,
She would be a long story book!

She is my mummy.

Stephanie Gardiner (8)
Colston's Lower School

MUSIC

I love to go to my music lessons,
And my half-hour piano sessions.
I love to listen to the beat,
It gets the rhythm in my feet.
I love to sing to the play,
'It's very good,' some will say.
I love to play on the keyboard,
Making sure I hit the right chord.
When the bell is ringing,
It's time to stop singing.

Jaime Bracewell (11)
Colston's Lower School

THE FURNITURE GAME

She would be a tidy set of drawers
She would be a bright morning
She would be a gorgeous guitar
She would be a lovely lasagne
She would be a crazy cartoon
She would be a super S Club 7
She would be a great gymnast
She would be a dainty dolphin
She would be some jumping jeans
She would be romantic Rome
She would be a sleek sports car.

It's Ruth!

Briony Brockhurst (8)
Colston's Lower School

A MUM'S POCKET

A handkerchief for whipping out and wiping your face with.
Embarrassing baby photos to show your friends.
Receipts for school shirts,
A spare pair of pants!
Her unused cheque book,
An empty purse,
Car and spare house keys.
Spare laces for your shoes
A really hard book,
And a maths test to do at home!

Kerala Drew (9)
Colston's Lower School

NAPOLEON I

He would be a hatstand
And a bright sunny midday.
He would be a big thundering set of drums,
He would be a French croissant,
He would be a look at his life,
And a cool rock band.
He would be a fast racer in cars,
He would be a wily fox,
He would be a trampling boot,
And a great exhibition over Europe.
He's a huge wagon
And a history book!

George Downs-Wheeler (9)
Colston's Lower School

THE CHEETAH

The cheetah.
It's as fast as light.
It's strong, small and furious.
Like a yellow light dashing through a field.
Like a speeding sound.
It makes me feel slow
Like a tortoise.
The cheetah,
Me the slow snail.

Brijesh Patel (10)
Colston's Lower School

THE RUGBY MATCH

Bone breaking
Mud disaster
Hooker hooking
Watchers staring
Rain flowing
Ball throwing
Try scoring!
Seven-nil
Drop goal
Ten-nil
Whistle gone
We won!

Rugby!

Robert Eden (8)
Colston's Lower School

WHAT YOU WOULD FIND
IN A SINGER'S POCKET

A radio to make them sing better,
A microphone to make them sing louder,
A magic sweet to stop them from being nervous,
A little person to tell them the words
And a special thing to push them to go the
right way for dance steps.

Aisha Ali (8)
Colston's Lower School

MY KITTEN

My kitten is so sweet
It's my mum's birthday treat,
It plays with the ball
And runs in the hall.

When I go to school
And sing in the hall,
I think about my cat
Sleeping on the mat.

When she scratches
At night, she has a fright.
The poor little cat.

My little cat.

Jack Maddox (10)
Colston's Lower School

THE POLAR BEAR

The polar bear
Roams free in its wild, white, wilderness.
Strong, stately, fierce,
Like a large snowdrop.
Like a snowball rolling freely;
It makes me feel weak,
Like a defenceless mouse.
The polar bear
Reminds me of my own strength.

Karl Hurkett (11)
Colston's Lower School

JOSH

He would be an armchair and a bright morning.
If he was a musical instrument,
He would be a loud trumpet.
He would be a sweet!
And if he was a TV programme
He would be a cartoon.
He is Limp Bizkit
A rugby ball, a tiger!
If he was a holiday, he would be a hot one!
If he was a form of transport
He would be an aeroplane.
He's a baggy pair of jeans
And a horrible history book!

Hamish FitzHenry (9)
Colston's Lower School

MY COUSIN JOE

He would be a fine leather sofa,
He would be midnight.
He would be a guitar and a roast dinner.
He would be the musical Kerrang
And the bashing Nirvana.
He would be the kick in football
And the snapping crocodile.
He would be an alien workshop T-shirt
And downhill mountain biking
He would be a Land Rover
And if he was a book, he would be Horrible Histories.

Samuel Ford (8)
Colston's Lower School

GEORGE

He would be a running machine,
He would be a daytime person,
He would be a squeaky violin,
He would be a hot dog with tomato sauce.
He would be a Tom and Jerry cartoon
And if he were a pop band he would be Five.
He would be jazzy clothes
And a footballer.
He would be a very fast cheetah,
He would be stretchy kind of clothes
And if he were a vehicle he would be a motorbike
If he were a book it would be a warrior book.
It's George!

David Huggins (8)
Colston's Lower School

ALLITERATION

One day we won a wicked water slide.
Two bad tempered televisions talked to each other.
Three thoughtful people threw out their thermal vests.
Four fat fishes had a festivity at four o'clock in the morning.
Five funny flamingos fluttered away.
Six sleepy security people slept through their jobs.
Seven people went shopping for sixty hours then slept.
Eight eggs excitedly cracked open.
Nine nannies knitted Nike shirts.
Ten talking tomatoes talked to a tiger.

Rowan Henry (9)
Colston's Lower School

THE FURNITURE GAME

She is a prowling tiger,
But on a cold day
She becomes a warm fleece.
A middle of the day active person,
She performs to the world
As a banging base drum.
She's a yummy hot pizza
And a mad cartoon.
She stands tall as a beautiful
Leather stool.
If she were a book
She would be a fairy tale.

She's Briony!

Henry Lowrey (8)
Colston's Lower School

MY MUM

She's a bouncy waterbed
And a bright sunny day.
She's a twinkling harp,
She is a salad,
She is a news show,
She is Mozart,
She's a swimmer.
She would be a sparkling dolphin.
She is a glittering dress,
She is a sunbathing holiday.
She would be a hang-glider.
She's a novel!

Joshua Harris (8)
Colston's Lower School

MATHEMATICS POEM

My desk is in the middle
I'm stuck there every day.
Mr Barber teaches me
In his very special way.
Add, subtract, times, divide
Will make me feel glad
But fractions
They really drive me mad!
He gives me long multiplication
My hand is in the air,
'Sir do you understand
I'm still waiting here!'
He gives me so much homework
I don't know where to start
I wish I wasn't sat in maths
I'd like to be in Art!

Rebecca Welling (9)
Colston's Lower School

THE FURNITURE GAME

She would be a comfy bed,
A night-time girl.
She's a smooth delicate violin,
She is tasty pizza
She's a 'jeany' person
She would be 'Blue Peter'
She would be S Club 7.
She is a cheetah,
She is a sandcastle
A wild animal book
And a casual sports car!

Annie Krawiec (8)
Colston's Lower School

CATHERINE WHEEL ACROSTIC!

C lashing, crashing,
A rk-shaped, exploding like bombs
T rashing, lashing noises
H ear the explosions go bang!
E choing round
R oar, roar, and roar
I nterstellar star wars going on
N ovember the 5th, November the 5th
E nding, ending

W onder when the wheel will end
H issing, hissing
E ver circling
E ver ending
L asting forever in our minds!

Anthony McLean (8)
Colston's Lower School

FOUND IN A MERMAID'S PURSE . . .

A droplet of the dark blue sea,
Fishes that have never been discovered before,
Ten thousand pearls that have been dancing in the sea,
The shiniest shells, pink, purple and blue,
A pet sea horse singing,
Shiny pebbles made into mirrors,
Pearl combs, the shiniest ever,
An abandoned bucket and spade,
The smoothest grain of sand ever found . . .

Aishah Masood (9)
Colston's Lower School

I'M HAPPY!

Boredom is when there's nothing to do,
Happiness is when your favourite song is on.
Boredom is when you're in the car going to school,
Happiness is blue sea,
Boredom is the black night sky,
Happiness is green grass,
Boredom is a grey foggy day,
Happiness is an orange evening sky,
Boredom is a brown tree,
Happiness is a white, whiteboard.
Happiness is red lips!

Michael Parrott (9)
Colston's Lower School

WITHOUT MY MUM

Without my mum I would be . . .

An omelette without egg,
A book without a name,
A mouse without cheese,
A tree without leaves,
A house without windows,
A teacher without children,
A hospital without doctors,
A bird without wings

So without my mum I am nothing at all.

Isabelle Pollitt (8)
Colston's Lower School

SUN AND WIND

Shining rays
It plays
Hot beams
Burning screams
Sun tan
Need fans!

Air blower
Mischief flower
Stone mover
Sucking Hoover
Cooling down
Blowing clowns
Uplifting air
I stare at the wind . . .

Joshua Olpherts-Forrester (9)
Colston's Lower School

A KENNING

Nut pincher
High climber
Cheeky smiler
Fruit eater
Furry faced
Long reacher
Banana lover
Never hover
Always moving
Never stopping.

A monkey!

Michael Whyard (8)
Colston's Lower School

I LIKE . . .

I like my friends,
I like my Game Boy,
I like my school,
I like my mum and dad,
I like my teacher,
I like my bedroom,
I like my Lego.

I don't like slugs,
I don't like Mondays,
I don't like lies,
I don't like to shout,
I don't like to be wet!

Matthew Bown (9)
Colston's Lower School

A KENNING

Song singer
Joy bringer
Ant attacker
Worm catcher
Food snatcher
Wheat eater
Message sender
Nest mender.

A dove.

Jeevan Singh (8)
Colston's Lower School

MISS THINKS

Miss thinks I'm listening
To her boring history tales
But I'm on an adventure
Looking for lots of nature
Swimming through the murky swamp
Where the frogs jump.

Miss thinks I'm reading
Oh no, she's wrong
I'm on an adventure
Searching for gold
Climbing trees and being bold
What's the matter? I'm feeling cold.

Miss thinks I'm working,
But no,
I'm on an adventure,
I'm soaring through the air like a bird,
I'm flying into the air,
High above the trees and high above the bumblebees.

Amy Wates (10)
Colston's Lower School

THE FURNITURE GAME

He is a very bright morning and quite a drum kit!
He is a Happy Meal and quite a tough rugby game,
He is a black leather shirt and a lion,
He would be a stretch limo.
He's Henry!

Zak Bond (9)
Colston's Lower School

MISS THINKS

Mrs Webley thinks I am working hard but . . .

I am playing rugby for my school team,
We beat them easy - sixty-ten,
I am now having something to eat with them,
I am now going on the coach back to school,
The coach was late by half an hour,
I wonder what my mum and dad are
Going to think about this?

Mrs Webley thinks I am reading my book but . . .

I am swimming in the sea in Jamaica,
I am then surrounded by sharks,
I try to think clever,
They then come at me,
I dive under just in time,
The sharks bang together loudly,
I am safe at last,
I swim to shore.

Buster Lawrence (10)
Colston's Lower School

FLUTE

The flute is a rather long strange thing
It looks like a tree where monkeys swing.
Its buttons are like mole holes.
The high note, around it rolls
Its colour shines in the light
Like a street lamp ever so bright.
The flute is as light as a feather
It will go on playing forever and ever.

Chloe Scudamore (11)
Colston's Lower School

TIME TO CALL IN GROUND FORCE

For as long as I can remember,
The garden has always been there.
In front of the path to our garage,
Nothing fancy, exotic or rare.

Just a large plot of vegetables growing,
In tidy neat rows end to end,
The old men who tenderly dug there,
An old villager and his friend.

I remember sprout stalks stiff like soldiers,
Tall bean canes entwined with red flowers.
Potatoes and carrots abounded,
They laboured for hours and hours.

When one of the gardeners suddenly died,
The other struggled on for a time.
He tried hard to keep the plants growing,
But sadly it was the end of the line.

The cabbage patch turned to a wilderness,
A haven for birds, full of seeds,
Long gone were the beautiful show winners,
Now a few rogue shoots in the weeds.

A 'For Sale' sign appeared one wet Wednesday,
On the gatepost at the side of the lane,
My mum and dad said 'Such a pity,
Will it ever be a garden again?'

We really didn't need two gardens,
But the space would be useful for Dad.
He enjoys growing plants and digging,
So we decided to do something mad.

Our offer to buy was accepted
And it's ours at the end of the week,
I can't wait to help rebuild the walls,
The cost I admit was quite steep . . .

For a compost heap!

William Gallimore (11)
Colston's Lower School

MY UNDERWATER WORLD

When ever I go swimming in the deep blue sea,
As a mermaid you may find me.

All the treasure is shimmering gold,
It stands out for miles, bright and bold.

Necklaces, bracelets, tiaras too,
There are so many, I mean what can I do?

Fancy dress party,
Posh and smarty.

Kings and queens fit for a ball,
Really now I have got it all.

I swim with dolphins in shimmering blue,
I wish I could stay here alone with you.

Walking on the shore paddling in the sea,
Here alone just you and me.

Emma Fredericks (8)
Colston's Lower School

MRS IAN

Mrs Ian thinks I'm drawing,
But I'm in a speed boat trying to win a race,
I'm in a World Cup football match
And I've scored two goals,
I'm the first boy to walk on Mars.

Mrs Ian thinks I'm writing my story,
But I'm fighting a crocodile,
Then its mouth snaps shut!
I'm watching a racing car race
And four of the cars flip over.

Mrs Ian thinks I'm reading my book well,
But I'm busy jumping off a cliff,
A hundred and fifty foot deep,
I'm the World Champion of motor cross.

Warren Abrahams (9)
Colston's Lower School

WEATHER

My dogs sit looking out of the window.
Tipple, topple, drizzle goes the rain,
Bang, clash, roar goes the thunder,
Crackle, flash, swish goes the lightning.

My dogs sit looking into the sparkling fire.
The flames were dancing,
The black burning coal was melting away,
My dogs snuggled up and snored.

Matthew Narey (9)
Colston's Lower School

DREAMS

Miss thinks I'm writing at work,
But I'm playing music with Louis Armstrong,
Swimming all the way to France,
Being the best at a celebrity dance,
Flying with Superman,
Even with x-ray vision,
I'm on a battlecruiser for an army mission.
Miss thinks I'm filling in my record
But I'm wrestling for the world,
Hitting someone out the window with a carpet curled.
So why can't that, it is me,
Why can't everyone let me be!

Julian Walcott-Gordon (9)
Colston's Lower School

HARMONICA

The harmonica is a very small instrument,
That responds to every blow or breeze.
The sound is like a squeaky mouse
That looks like a short thick twig.

It is very difficult to play,
Maybe because it's so small.
The notes vary from high to low.
Whatever goes on inside it,
I just do not know.

Sam Gardiner (11)
Colston's Lower School

MY DAYDREAM

Miss thinks I'm reading
But I'm running to win the game
Then I'm racing and see the flame
But I bet I'll get the blame.

Miss thinks I'm listening
But I'm in the park
Playing with my friends, Bill, Fred and Mark
Kicking round a football until I hear a dog bark.

Miss thinks I'm writing
But I'm swimming in the sea
Hoping that the shark doesn't eat me for his tea
Suddenly I hear my name, oh dear it's Miss calling me!

James Cloake (9)
Colston's Lower School

OUTER SPACE

Millions of glittering stars suspended there in orbit,
The glowing face of the moon smirking down here on us,
All the bright stars are fast asleep whereas comets zoom and whiz,
The astronomers look up into the dark night sky
And watch the time go by.
All the aliens and the other creatures look
Down on us on Earth,
Shooting stars travelling from here over to Mars
And me staring up there at the wonderful face
Of the luminous moon.

Esther Carter (9)
Colston's Lower School

THE TREASURE

Dive deep,
Where dark things sleep,
To find the treasure heap.

He hears no sound,
As he swims to the ground,
He sees a wreck,
What has he found?

He swims inside and sees the treasure,
He knows it is the end of his adventure.

He takes the gold to the shore and is rich for evermore.

Philip Box (8)
Colston's Lower School

MY BED

In my bed
I lay my sleepy head.
I like to listen to the rain
As it bangs on my window frame.
I like to think I'm in the water -
Or I am a rich man's daughter!
Or I'm on a cloud going round and round,
In soft white fluff looking down at the ground.
People below are unaware
That from my cloud down I stare
Until I float into another dream . . .
Don't wake me. That's too mean!

Jayne Hulin (11)
Colston's Lower School

UNDERWATER ADVENTURE

There was a boy called Ben
He went underwater.
A little fish swam past his head
And in his hand he caught her.

There was a boy called Ben
He went underwater.
Shrimps swam by and he swished them away.
Jellyfish came by and he made them jump!

There was a boy called Ben
He went underwater.
He saw a whale 50 metres long
Who tried to gobble him up,
But instead it swallowed a stone.

Anthony But (11)
Colston's Lower School

ROSE

My friend Rose is very clever
I'll be her best friend for ever and ever
When I'm feeling down
She comes to me and eases my frown
She likes eating lots of food
But she is hardly ever rude
She is always smiling and always fun
But now I'm afraid that my poem is done.

Claire Whyard (9)
Colston's Lower School

THE HIDDEN TREASURE

I'm about to dive into the deep blue sea,
To search for treasure just for me.
In I go with a great big splash,
I'm very excited so I swim with a dash.
It's very misty and cold and dark,
I spot the treasure but then the shark!
I hide in the rocks with my eyes shut tight,
I hope the shark won't come to bite.
It swims away, there's no time to play.
Now's my chance!
I move like a sea horse
And jump with a prance,
I come up from the water onto the sand,
I'm glad to get my treasure back on the land.

Jacob Nowak (7)
Colston's Lower School

A HOCKEY MATCH

The whistle blows,
The games begin,
She's got the ball,
She hits it in!
The team all cheer,
The referee blows,
The whistle once again.
Then the ball is hit,
Up to the other end.
Will they score?
Oh no! They have.

Rebecca Helps (11)
Colston's Lower School

A Sad Christmas Poem

There was a little boy
Who in his life didn't have a lot of joy.
But he waited and waited for Christmas Day to come.
Although he didn't have a lot of fun.
He said, 'I still have a Christmas tree
The size of me.'

The stars shone in the sky
Bright and high
As the angels flew by.
They prayed as they waited
For the little boy to have
Joy.

Aimee Marshall (9)
Colston's Lower School

By Sea

By sea I'm searching,
Deep, deep down in the oceans below.

The lobsters, the crabs,
The ruins, the seaweed.

I swim inside the ruin,
Oh dear, there's a shark!

Luckily he did not see me,
There is a clown fish,
Now that's what I call treasure.

Samuel Crew (8)
Colston's Lower School

POOH AND HIS FRIENDS

Pooh, so big, round and yellow,
Playing with his friends,
Kanga, Piglet, Rabbit and Roo.

Tigger bouncing up in the sky,
Thinking he can fly,
Eeyore the donkey with a tail so wonky.

These are the friends,
Kanga, Piglet, Rabbit and Roo,
Tigger and Eeyore and not forgetting Pooh.

Jessica-Leigh Warboys (8)
Colston's Lower School

OUTER SPACE

One cheesy moon hovering in outer space,
Millions of flashing stars with a smiley face,
The biggest black hole whizzing wondrously,
The huge comets bumping constantly.

The enormous earth blocking out the light,
As all the asteroids move steadily in the night,
Hundreds of shooting stars zooming by,
Then we come to aliens -
Everyone's scared of them, but why?

Rachel Ellis (9)
Colston's Lower School

THE MATCH

Getting close,
The fans stand up,
It's getting tense,
As the ball is shot,
The ball goes high,
It comes back down
And in the net,
The keeper sighs,
The whistle is blown,
And it's six to five,
The coach is pleased,
With his six goal side.

Christopher Maggs (9)
Colston's Lower School

SNOWSTORM

The white wind of whirling snow
Gives us a fright.
People exclaim, 'It's quite a sight!'
Children go out to play in the snow.
When they come back their faces glow,
The sun comes out
And melts the thick snow
And turns it into a big puddle.

Thomas Gollop (11)
Colston's Lower School

UNDER THE SEA

Under the sea, dive down very deep,
To find the hidden treasure for you to keep.
You will see fish and whales,
You might even see a crab with big claws.
I swim through seaweed, seashells and
I have found the treasure,
Gold and silver.

Claire Aldridge (8)
Colston's Lower School

HAPPINESS IS . . .

When I win a game,
When my dad falls for a trick,
When it is maths,
When I play with my friends,
When everything goes well.

Disappointment is Monday!

Ashley Blackmore (9)
Colston's Lower School

MY HERO COLIN

The racing driver I like best
Is one called Colin McRae.
He races away through thick and thin,
Dashing through weather, trying to win.
Racing round corners, whizzing round bends,
Trying to make it all the way to the end.

Adam Watkins (11)
Colston's Lower School

BENEATH THE CORAL

Beneath the coral, the treasure lies,
Old and gold piled up high,
Shining bright in every way,
Seeking through the rocks of fright,
You will find it by night.

Nicole Hutson (8)
Colston's Lower School

THE UNLUCKY CAT

I jumped over
The fence,
The fence,
To see what the horrible
Noise was.
The cat was running up the
Tree,
The tree,
Scratching all the bark off,
The dog was running
After the cat
And he gobbled him in one
Go,
Luckily he didn't notice
Me,
Behind the tree,
The tree.

Lewis Amos (10)
Courtney Primary School

UNDER THE SEA

It's amazing under the sea,
Just to watch all the fish,
I'd like to go under the sea,
Just to see all the fish,
I'd stop all the oil,
Just to see all the beautiful fish,
Red fish,
Yellow fish,
Pink fish,
It'd be lovely to go under the sea,
Just to see all the fish,
I'd stop all the oil,
Just to see all the fish!

Sophie Gallant (10)
Courtney Primary School

THE HORSE RACE

Trot, trot,
Gallop, gallop,
Let that horse go off the track.

See that rider,
Control that horse
She should win the Golden Cup.

I wish I could
Ride like that tonight
With her.

Neigh, neigh.

Paige Frere (10)
Courtney Primary School

WOULD YOU LIKE TO BE!

Would you like to be,
A giraffe,
Dining at the tallest tree!

Would you like to be,
An eagle,
Soaring wild and free!

Would you like to be,
A dolphin,
Swimming in a turquoise sea!

Would you like to be,
A tiger,
With stripes so bright!

Would you like to be,
A horse,
To gallop along with me!

Would you like to be,
A chimpanzee,
Who shares human thoughts!

Would you like to be,
A human,
A girl or a boy!

Rebecca McLaughlin (10)
Courtney Primary School

THE SNAKE

The silver slimy snake slithers
Out of his snug house,
Searching for his scrumptious meal,
Underneath the starlight bright.

He adores seeing all the strong animals,
While he's searching for his food,
When he's found his food,
He slithers back home for his feast of mice!

Jade Gregory (9)
Courtney Primary School

THE SEA OF TREASURE

The sea that night was a raging monster,
Tearing up everything in its path,
The sea thundered out and tore back in,
This was a night of doom.

From the window, I could see a blood-stained wall,
Just as the sea swept out,
The wall was grey and strong and tall
And in big red letters it spelt,
There is a treasure in this sea.

The very next day, I swam out to sea,
Finding a map in the rocks,
A map for gold, a map for a ship,
I must find this I thought.

One day five years later, I travelled
To sea in a boat,
I saw the treasure and dived deep down,
This is the treasure I want, I thought,
Yes this is the treasure I want.

That very day I became rich,
Without having to search down a dirty ditch,
I had some gold and a ship,
Now forever I'd be rich.

Hannah Britton (10)
Courtney Primary School

THE LIVING STONE

Golden welcoming gates,
That show the entrance to the cave,
With frightening sturdy statues,
In the shape of men.

The dark dismal cave,
With trickling water,
That gleams in the light,
Coming from a source.

The fiery torch leads the way,
Into the cave,
Something golden and glittering,
A stone that fills the cave with light,
The living stone.

The living stone,
Gives you eternal life,
No matter what happens to you,
Everyone tries to seize the treasure,
But they have never succeeded.

Daniel Marks (10)
Courtney Primary School

THE SNAKE

S   lavering snake,
N   ibbling on the petrified rodent,
A   nimals fear the slavering snake,
K   nife-like yellow, poisonous fangs,
E   dible he is, but no one dares to eat him.

Jake Beesley (9)
Courtney Primary School

HIDDEN TREASURE

H idden beneath the ocean shore,
I n a chest deep down low,
D umped by someone of course, now poor,
D own beneath the ocean blue,
E xplorers have gone but not once found it,
N o one's seen it except sea creatures.

T oo slippery to pick up, never mind to hold,
R uined ships, dead people's skeletons,
E aten by sharks, eaten by sea creatures,
A t the sight of treasure, at the sight of death,
S hips rotting away, disappearing out of sight,
U nder a few old rocks and stones,
R ipped up clothes and broken bones,
E lectric eels helped me out but in the end
gave me a shock.

Katerina Schwemin (10)
Courtney Primary School

BIRTH STONES

Amethyst, as purple as a carnation,
Jade, as green as leaves,
Sapphire, as blue as the sky.

Ruby, is as red as a rose,
Pearl, as white as an ice cream,
Crystal, as shiny as the moon.

These are all the birth stones,
Which one is yours?

Rebecca Thomas (10)
Courtney Primary School

THE JOURNEY

I dreamed of a journey of life,
Which took me 10,000 miles,
The task was to get on a plane and
To sit down and enjoy the ride.

When I got to the forest of trees,
I found a place that was just known to me,
I went inside guess what to find?
Some bright treasure like me.

Before I could get it, a roar collided
With my ear drum,
It was a green dragon with blue scales,
With claws the size of King Kong,
I picked up a stick and lit it,
As it slowly burned the dragon suddenly turned,
So I grabbed for the treasure,
Which gave me plenty of pleasure,
So I took it and ran.

James Souch (10)
Courtney Primary School

MY DRAGON

My dragon is mighty,
My dragon is dangerous,
My dragon is friendly,
My dragon is great,
My dragon has red scales,
My dragon has green wings,
My dragon is the best.

Daniel Smullen (9)
Courtney Primary School

HIDDEN TREASURE

In a dark, damp cave
Lies a ring of eternal life,
But guarding it for eternity,
A Cyclops as old as the earth.

Many have tried and tried,
But none have succeeded,
None of them knew the secret,
Of the enchanted chest.

The only way to open it,
Is the golden key,
Slay the Cyclops, open his heart,
Inside you will find the key.

Ross Dicks (11)
Courtney Primary School

MY GOLDFISH

My fish he lives in a bowl,
He swims,
He eats
And then he sleeps,
What's the point of a goldfish?
They are as much point as a stone,
What's the point?
What's the point?
What's the point of a goldfish?

Ashley Mark Staples (10)
Courtney Primary School

HIDDEN TREASURE

Deep beneath the ocean bed,
Lies a ship all covered in fish,
While the scuba-divers search,
All the fish are swimming around.

In the distance, they see a chest,
Around it they see that it's gleaming,
They swim to it, as fast as they can,
When they get near it, they have a shock.

When they open the chest,
They see a flash of light,
They get their scuba pockets
And frighten off the fish.

Then they float up to the surface
And put things in their boat,
They show their master the treasure
And then go back for more.

Lauren Hardwell (10)
Courtney Primary School

THE DANGEROUS DRAGON

The dangerous dragon,
Plods along like thunder,
Its body has glowing red, razor scales,
Its teeth are like chain saws,
His feet are like mighty rocks,
His very powerful wings are
Like helicopter blades,
His claws are like shark's teeth
But he's the friendliest thing around.

Scott Bowden (10)
Courtney Primary School

HIDDEN TREASURE

As I was sailing in the ocean one day,
I saw a box under the sea,
I reached and reached but could not touch
And then I had an idea,
I jumped underwater
And swam and swam
And then touched,
My fingertips went cold,
But then it opened,
Inside of this box was gold, silver,
Gems, jewels and a ring,
The ring was now mine,
This ring was the world,
I now owned the world.

Georgina Rogers (11)
Courtney Primary School

HIDDEN TREASURE

Treasure beneath the ocean,
Rotting with rust around the lock,
Explorers tried to find it but didn't succeed,
At night it is all quiet and the chest is still there,
So many people tried but didn't get it,
Under the water, the best is hidden,
Rotting even more day by day,
One day somebody might find it,
Who will it be?

Zoe Cole (10)
Courtney Primary School

THE HIDDEN CHAMBER

Writing on the bottom of my shed,
Led me to an unusual place.

I found a chamber under the sea,
Full of golden sweets and chocolate.

Pearls and pure gold and silver,
Hidden in the chamber of secrets.

This area of the sea is restricted
But people have dared to dive.

Deep down guarding the treasure is a dragon,
As fierce as a giant flame.

People who have dared to dive
Never returned again.

Should I dare to dive in deep,
Deep through the ocean blue?

Should I dare to fight
The thundering dragon?

Should I risk my life
To get through the chamber?

Do I dare? Do I dare?

Zoe Hoare (10)
Courtney Primary School

MY FIRE DRAGON

My fire dragon sprints along all day,
Through his lit up cave,
For his tea, he eats fish and chips,
From the river and lake,
His pointy scales are as sharp as they can get.

He rocks and rocks around all day,
Wanting someone to play with him,
He's really friendly,
He's really great,
My fire dragon is my bestest friend.

Charles Pope (9)
Courtney Primary School

THE TREASURE OF LIFE

In a bricked up house
In an attic,
The spirit protects the treasure of life,
The treasure of life,
The treasure of life.
It keeps anyone alive forever
And ever.

Up and down the corridors,
A spirit roams for evermore,
There he goes, working hard
He does it well, oh yes he does.

Spirit, spirit, guard my treasure
Protect it well and you'll have pleasure.

I bet you will love hunting people,
That is what your pleasure is.

Tiana Rosser (11)
Courtney Primary School

HIDDEN TREASURE

One day my dad told me,
That once he threw a chest of
Treasure in the sea,
When he was a little boy.

The big brown chest has been
Undiscovered since 1973.
A big, old, rotten oak tree standing still,
Doing nothing but knowing the map
Buried three steps away is about to be discovered.

On Friday after school, we're going down,
To defeat this shark,
On Friday we meet the angry sea,
That crashes and roars.

A mean, unfriendly shark guards the gems,
The shark's sharp teeth were as white as snow,
Nobody dared to tackle him,
Until now.

We found the key on the hook,
So we opened it up to see what
Was inside and it was . . .
Beautiful, sparkly gems of all
The colours of the rainbow.

Abbie-Leigh Hayes-Collier (10)
Courtney Primary School

TREASURE ISLAND

Once there was a map which was found
And there was gold which was hidden,
But it was booby-trapped all around,
On an island which was forbidden.

It was forbidden because it was too dangerous,
For playing games like chase,
There were things that were very monstrous,
It was a very frightening place.

Helen Waddington (11)
Courtney Primary School

HIDDEN TREASURE - THE MAP

In a dark, damp dungeon,
Far, far away,
Lies a treasure map,
To seek one day.

Opening a rusty door,
Leading to a lonely passage,
Getting an ever bigger key,
To a castle door.

In the deserted castle,
On the chamber floor,
A map will lie forever
And evermore.

If someone ever finds it,
All their wishes will come true,
There'll be a puff of magic smoke
And the map will be gone.

Amy McFarland (10)
Courtney Primary School

DEEP BENEATH THE OCEAN

Deep beneath the ocean, cold,
Lives the treasure which is old,
Guarded by the sea creatures,
They're so scary, they're like dragons.

The sea is dark,
With a ferocious shark,
The treasure is silver and gold,
It's precious to the king.

Whoever tries to find it
And I don't think they ever will,
But . . . if you try and find the closely
Guarded treasure,
You should prepare to die.

Nicholas Challis (10)
Courtney Primary School

THE DOOR

Shiny glass bit in the middle,
Shining on the floor,
The turning handle like a mouth,
Opening the door.

On the side
A great big lock,
Fat and mighty, tall,
Be careful, you might get a shock,
Half connected to the wall!

Fiona Clabon (9)
Courtney Primary School

HIDDEN TREASURE

Far away in the deep, dark cave,
Lives some hidden treasure.
People try to capture it, but
Never get the pleasure.
When they get there,
They hear a monster roar,
So they always stay about
5 metres from the door,
They never go in, in case of
What might happen,
They could get eaten, burnt
Or even flattened.

Charlotte Skuse (11)
Courtney Primary School

HIDDEN TREASURE

Hidden treasure in the sea,
But you need a golden key,
Try to look and you might find,
The hidden treasure of one kind.

I searched, I searched, I could not see,
The hidden treasure of my destiny,
Oh key, oh key please come to me,
I've searched for all these years,
But the key is long lost.

Mitchel Whittaker (11)
Courtney Primary School

DOWN BELOW THE DEEP BLUE SEA

Down below the deep blue sea,
Is where gold treasures, well might be,
Hidden by some mystical creature,
Hiding all that golden treasure,
Hidden slightly beyond the sand,
That's far away from our land,
Down below the deep blue sea,
Is where gold treasures, well might be.

Ayasha Rahman (10)
Courtney Primary School

RICH TREASURE

Deep under the wavy ocean bed,
Lies a massive treasure chest,
The sunken ship hides all the jewels,
The tattered pirates search for precious treasure.

Gold, silver, bronze and all,
The richest treasure with all the jewels,
It glows in the dark and sparkles in the day,
Get past the ship and you might be rich.

Jamie Siddell (11)
Courtney Primary School

TREASURE

T   reasure buried under the sea,
R   usted round the rotten edges,
E   nclosed in a heap of sand,
A   sea monster guards it very closely,
S   ilver and gold, coins and cups,
U   nder the seabed,
R   agged wood protects the gold,
E   merged after a hundred years.

Nial Emes (10)
Courtney Primary School

THE UNDISCOVERED TREASURE

In a crusty cave hidden under plants,
A mysterious dragon guards a lot of treasures,
The glittering jewels dazzle anyone who comes near,
So the precious riches will be safe for a long time,
The deep, dark forest nearby, holds secrets,
The king's strong soldiers march to the cave,
'Oh dear the treasure isn't safe.'

Kirsty Lewis (10)
Courtney Primary School

THE DRAGON

The moon is as beautiful as a dragon's eye,
The cloud is like the dragon's smoke,
The raindrops are like the dragon's tears,
The sun is as bright as the dragon's fire.

Gemma Lucas (9)
Courtney Primary School

DEEP BENEATH THE OCEAN

Deep beneath the ocean, treasure lies shining,
The sunken ship wrecked in the war,
The colourful fish shimmering,
The clear, wavy ocean glistening in the light,
The mouldy rocks sunk in the sand,
The slimy seaweed floating out from the ground,
The gold and silver treasure all glistening in the light.

Jade Belton (11)
Courtney Primary School

MY PET DRAGON

My pet dragon,
Has red, hot fire,
His eyes are as big as footballs,
His ears are as sharp as razor blades,
White, shiny teeth,
Green polished scales.

Amy Ford (10)
Courtney Primary School

HIDDEN TREASURE

Under the clear wavy sea sits a golden chest,
The colourful fish swim around the glistening jewels,
The sunken ship lies all alone on the seabed,
The worn-out pirates search for the long lost treasure,
The glittery, shiny treasure sparkles in the dark night.

Penny Lyons (11)
Courtney Primary School

HIDDEN TREASURE

An old crusty house sits on the edge of a street,
Dusty and empty, it stands there alone,
But it hides a secret room,
Which is an attic with spiders and cobwebs
In the corners,
Gold and shiny, treasure lies there waiting
For someone to come along,
And unlock the dark secret.

Jayde Holcombe (10)
Courtney Primary School

HIDDEN TREASURE

Deep inside a gloomy cave,
Sleeps a dragon day by day.

Guarding treasure each day and night,
Treasure gleams shining bright.

Treasure hiding in a room,
Gold and silver, a treat for all.

Aaron Thorne (10)
Courtney Primary School

EGYPTIAN TREASURE

In Egypt there's a pyramid, that has never been found,
Inside there's a maze, which twists round and round,
If you pass it, you get to beautiful things,
Such as gold, statues, bracelets and rings,
But you have to get out quick from the room,
Or the door will shut and you'll be stuck in the tomb.

Carrie Manning (11)
Courtney Primary School

THE PLAYGROUND

The big gold bell's eyes twinkle in the sunshine,
As the benches wouldn't keep still,
It was like they had ants in their pants,
The massive door glass was shining
From the twinkling moon,
The big grey steps were staring peeringly
At the big dull playground,
Where the benches were riding
Around and the climbing frame
Was falling to the ground,
When the children climbed on top of it.

Joelene Bishop (11)
Crockerne CE Primary School

SCENE FROM A PLAYGROUND

The windows grin all day and all night,
While the street lights sleep in all day,
The old rotten fences cough in the polluted air,
As the greenhouse listens to the young birds quarrel.
The benches chuckle as the grass scratches them,
The old smelly litter bin eats up all the children's fruit.
Every old wooden door screeches at the gleaming
New cars that go past,
Washing lines slither on the bumpy concrete.

Katie Bunce (11)
Crockerne CE Primary School

SCENE FROM A PLAYGROUND

Washing lines grin as the wall walks by,
The windows rattle as the bells ring,
The rooftops sing as the drainpipes dance.

Laura Matthews (11)
Crockerne CE Primary School

HIDDEN TREASURE

When families die, I think of them,
As hidden treasure because
They are there
But not seen
I sometimes laugh,
Sometimes cry,
With memories of where they have been
It is like
Taking a deep breath of fresh air
When special people die
I gain a bit of heart.

One of my best things is,
My grandad's light in the sitting room,
Because it reminds me of him,
But I have more family
Budding ahead of me.

Laura Wogan (8)
Fairfield School

HIDDEN TREASURE

The sunken galleon lies so deep,
The ghastly mast so tall and crooked.
Once that old wreck was the
Sturdiest ship that ever braved the Seven Seas.
Rioting with hundreds of storms,
But alas!
One storm lasted for days and thrashed the poor ship
Until it was into tiny bits,
Separated across the ocean
Like when a cat lands in a mouse family,
The mice scatter as quickly as
The parts of the ship scatter as the storm pounces on the ship.
But, that was years ago now,
It is rotting at the bottom of the sea.
But what do any other people know about it,
No one will ever discover the mysteries of the deep.

David Merfield (8)
Fairfield School

HIDDEN TREASURE

My heart is my treasure
It is more valuable than anything.
It's like fire, it's peaceful,
My heart gives me life,
Love.
Everyone has one deep inside them,
Some people just don't show it though.

Katherine Tomlinson (8)
Fairfield School

HIDDEN TREASURE

It is a tiny piece of snow
It's as if all of that frost goes into a snowman
And one unique snowflake landed on
My hand.
What do I do? I sigh,
I think, 'I wish I was a snowflake!'
The snowflake melted . . . I started to cry
I went inside to the house by the
Warm fire.
Mum came in, I told her everything
        The beautiful
        Snowflake.

Alex Horton (8)
Fairfield School

THE TORTOISE

The little tortoise is in its small shell,
Coming out on its first day
Takes very few steps
Then goes back in its tiny shell
It settles down
You never know what lies in there
It could be hidden treasure
He could have built a hole to put the treasure in
Inside is the mystery
That only one person knows
And that is . . .

Jake Miner (8)
Fairfield School

HIDDEN TREASURE

My hidden treasure is
Everywhere
It lives to
Help me and the animals.
It's like a *fireball* but
It helps the pipes of my body work,
It has a mind of its own.

My hidden treasure is deep down
In my body and
My hidden treasure is my heart.

It helps me feel
Love, happiness and kindness.
My heart is very special
I think of it as a huge
Beam of red light,
Like the sun rising and setting in the sky,
My heart beckons
With love and justice.

Polly Savva (9)
Fairfield School

HIDDEN TREASURE

Up in the sky
Clouds float slowly, silently
They float higher in the sky, like a bird,
There is no evil,
Just peace,
It is like a pure, shining, blue sea,
Where water is calm and peaceful.

Kathryn Law (8)
Fairfield School

HIDDEN TREASURES

Heaven is like a funfair,
With crystal walls and the rides
Best ever.
The noise is so loud,
It nearly deafens you
And everybody is so excited,
The largest merry-go-round
And fantastic stalls
And best of all, a home
For God and His son.

Matthew Organ (8)
Fairfield School

HIDDEN TREASURE

I float around in the sky
You use me every day.
Plants and animals use it too,
We live on it,
But it is not earth.
If it is trapped
It goes warm,
If it was fabric it would be silk!
It is a small breeze of warm air!
That's my hidden treasure.

Abbie Brace (9)
Fairfield School

HIDDEN TREASURES

There are many languages on this planet,
It is like a weaving with them all popping in and out,
English is a strong white,
Latin, gold and red,
German is a pale green and black,
French is blue and yellow,
Greek is a warm and happy silver,
Now the cloth is woven,
They're like lost people,
Sneaking around
And there are still more languages to come.

James Fox (8)
Fairfield School

HIDDEN TREASURES

How I would love to see the hidden treasures of the planets,
If I could hear them,
Mercury would be dull and grey,
Venus, soft fuzzy music,
Earth would be hip-hop,
Mars is the sound of war and blood,
Jupiter I think is classical,
Saturn must be modern,
Pluto, Uranus and Neptune are like where they come from,
Space.

James Cole (9)
Fairfield School

HIDDEN TREASURES

Heaven is a hidden treasure
It has no rain and evil,
I think Heaven is in another
Galaxy
And the walls are like blinding gold,
The ceiling is made of shiny copper
And the floor is magical silver,
The people are glimmering angels
And the wings are fragile and bright,
The clothes are like the paper
Of a crystal book.

Robert Fox (8)
Fairfield School

HIDDEN TREASURES

Down, down into the sea,
A ship sinks.
Jewellery floating from the rooms
While it drowns, sparkling like stars.
Ruby, crystal, diamond necklaces,
The boat breaks in half, like ripping paper.
It crashes, like an anchor dropping,
Bracelets getting dirty, as the sands cover them.
Down, down in the sea,
The Titanic sleeps.

Kimberley Tsang (8)
Fairfield School

HIDDEN TREASURES

They look like men with
Frozen shiny swords
Coming down to fight
The ground
White, frosty, crunchy, sparkly, soft,
Cold, peaceful, chilly, freezing,
Delicate,
I come out
In winter and people play
With me.
What am I?
A snowflake.

Billy Jukes (8)
Fairfield School

HIDDEN TREASURES

Space is as blue as the pure dangerous sea,
Cold, perilous.
If I go too deep into the sea,
It is risky.
The spacesuit is just like a diver's suit,
If I went too far into space,
I would feel far away from Earth,
Sad, but excited,
Missing my home.

Lloyd Morgan (8)
Fairfield School

HIDDEN TREASURES

Roman skulls have been found
But rarely any fossils
Some people have found coins, some helmets.
In a museum, you can find many things like
Helmets, swords and shields and armour.
Coins, stones and chariots.
The stones have writing on them.
I think the stones are gravestones
That have been attacked by other people,
But not Roman soldiers.

Chris Edis (9)
Fairfield School

HIDDEN TREASURE

Have you ever
Looked up to the sky
When the sun has changed to the moon?
As the crystal stars gleam in the velvety sky,
As the moon sends its golden beam,
When the comets speed past,
They lighten up the sky.

Eddie Obree (9)
Fairfield School

THE MAGIC BOX

I will put in my box,
The stare of a flashing camera,
An army of ants ready to fight,
The rings of Saturn in space glowing with gold.

I will put in my box,
A whistle with a wispy sound,
A pigeon perched on a person,
Three crimson roses with petals like silk.

I will put in my box,
The rattle of a rattlesnake,
A mellow feeling wanting to burst out!
A yawning clock with silver hands.

I will put in my box,
A witch's cackle echoing through my ears,
A squeak of a mouse,
A prowl of a tiger.

I will put in my box,
A lucky four-leaf clover, as green as the grass,
The waves of the deep blue sea crashing against the rocks.

My box is fashioned with gold and silver,
A rainbow across the top and hopes and wishes in the corners,
A 13th month and an octopus with twelve legs.

I will ride in my box and surf the waves,
Then I will be swept away to the shore,
Onto a golden beach filled with shells.

I will fly to the moon in my box, touch the surface of Mars,
Feel the tip of the moon, skim the edge of Venus,
And see the flicker of a comet's tail flying away.

Lisa Dark (10)
Fromebank Junior School

THE MAGIC BOX

I will put in my box . . .
The petite petal of a petrified pansy.
The glint of a young chameleon's eye.
The last beat of a heart.

I will put in my box . . .
The creak of solemn door.
The flick as you turn over a new leaf.
The puff of a tired steam train.

I will put in my box . . .
The crash of the World Trade Centre plummeting to the ground.
The ting of a pin landing on a pearly white floor.
The scratch of a young child's pencil.

I will put in my box . . .
The sound of a courageous army marching into battle.
A yawning grandfather clock with a cold.
The bottom lip of a tortoise.

My box is fashioned from dodo feathers.
The corners are the sharp orange tips of an owl's beak.
Hidden around the edges of my box are all of the
Colours of the rainbow.

In my box I will . . .
Stop world hunger, escape the jaws of a mighty giant
And ride away on a unicorn's back, with a horn from the
End of the world.

Emma Hill (10)
Fromebank Junior School

THE MAGIC BOX

I will put in my box
A buzzing bee dancing through the sky
A bouncing banana playing with a ball
A diamond that gives seven wishes.

I will put in my box
The bite of a boisterous book
The rigs of Saturn that fell from space
The lick of a lovely lolly.

I will put in my box
A leaping lama licking an ice lolly
A giggle from the statue of liberty
A chunk of chocolate singing a song.

My box is fashioned from
See-through glass with
Jewels in it
The hinges are made from bracelets.

I will sleep in my box
On a nice, comfy bed
Then I will swim with dolphins
I will play with my chocolate factory,
I will play my flute.

Kathryn Whiting (11)
Fromebank Junior School

I WILL PUT IN MY BOX . . .

I will put in my box a falling tower from New York
and people shouting for our help.
I will put in my box a twinkle of a snowflake on a Christmas night.
I will put in my box a postbox that can talk
and walk on the corner of my street.

I will put in my box the sound of a crash of glass shattering
and clattering to the ground.
My box is made from a tiger's hair and an eyeball,
also a sparkle of a clown's nose.

Benjamin Payne (11)
Fromebank Junior School

MY MYSTICAL DREAM BOX

I will put in my box . . .
The bad bite of a baffled book,
And the lost life of a living lion roaring at the sun.

I will put in my box . . .
The whispering whistle of the wild wind curving
Round the freezing Antarctic.

I will put in my box . . .
The fourth horn of a terrific triceratops,
Battling with the second Sunday in one week.

My box is created from . . .
The sizzling skin of a leaping lion,
And the warm fluff of a sheep's fleece.

My box will have . . .
Blue dreams dazzling the locks,
And dark ink drowning my worst fears.

In my box I will . . .
Carry a courageous cat while
I tango with a Tasmanian tiger in a tumour,
Then laze in a lumpy pool of custard.

Ellie Nichol (11)
Fromebank Junior School

THE MAGIC BOX

I will put in my box
An egg that gives the best wishes on Earth
A bee that gave the sharpest stings with a piercing scream
Which will be heard,
     heard.

I will put in my box
A bubbly blue balloon floating through the blue summer's day
The glassed stare from a beady amber eye,
       eye.

I will put in my box
A ping of spring that came from a wing
That gave ping a piecing part,
     part.

My box is fashioned from sparkling webs and hinges
And the words ting and ping
The dream of a child in the corners
And decorated with the colours of the rainbow
The dazzling diamonds on top of the lid,
      lid.

I will play in my box
The sweet sounding clarinet
    clarinet.

Amber L Ford (10)
Fromebank Junior School

I WILL PUT IN MY BOX

I will put in my box
The shine of an orange KTM zooming through my box
In my box there will be a chattering postbox from the corner
of my street
Lighting smashes into my box

The rubber rules his way through my box
The smelly gels will make my box smell lush
The World Trade Center falling down and the shaking of glass
The twinkle of a red nose.

Gavin Pearce (10)
Fromebank Junior School

THE MAGIC BOX

I will put in my box
The third eye of a human from outer space
An ancient evacuee from World War I that stares into people's
troublesome minds.

I will put in my box
A choking air vent from the bottom of a polar bear's stomach
A swishing of a summer sea
The foot of a fighting forest from far, far away.

I will put in my box
A no, no, no of a plump dodo's beak
A squirt of the ink from a pen made of air
The snigger of a starry summer's night.

My box is fashioned from
Wriggly worm eyes all the way from Mount Everest
The power of a long trained muscle forms the lock on my box
A lock to which I have the only key.

In my box I will form a plan to stop terrorism
And every type of destruction you can think of.

Matthew Pearson (10)
Fromebank Junior School

MY MYSTERIOUS BOX

I put in my box
A talking postbox with an orange tongue
A silent, stupid, secret agent.

I will put in my box
A mad monkey making money
A boy with two left feet.

I will put in my box
A laugh from a hyena
An American man that walks on all fours
And an Indian elephant that walks on two feet.

My box is fashioned
With eagle feathers that stick to animals' flesh
And has arguments in the corners.

I will explore the future in my box
I'll tell you the future, soon.

Sam Curry (10)
Fromebank Junior School

I WILL PUT IN MY BOX

A slither of a slippery snake surfing along the desert,
A tree with a crooked smile,
A tip of a sharp shark's fin.

I will have in my box
The howl of an unknown werewolf
The blue of the waterfall that belongs to the wizard
The heart of a shivering snowman.

I will put in my box
The cackle of a cowboy on a crooked broomstick
The whacking laugh of a witch on a wicked white horse.

I made my box out of
Sparkling petals of a flower
Silk of a spider's web
I shall sleep in my box and have special dreams of writing this poem.

Zoe Dunn (10)
Fromebank Junior School

COLOURS

Red, red, where is a red?
Red, red, lovely red
It's in the sun
Yellow, yellow, where is a yellow?
Yellow, yellow, bright yellow
It's in the colour of paper
Green, green, where is a green?
Green, green, grassy green
It's in the life
Blue, blue, where is a blue?
Blue, blue, favourite blue
It's in the sky
Colour, colour, where is a colour?
Colour, colour, many colours, many colours
They are in the rainbow.

Peter Kim (9)
Henbury Court Primary School

IT'S MY MUM

My pretty mum has dark blue eyes like the deep, dark, shiny sea
My pretty, tall mum has the prettiest smile
She is kind but sometimes bossy, who cares? She's my mum
My lovely mum likes to wear colourful clothes that suit her very much
Oh, my mum, she eats healthy food
She's pretty on the outside and she's pretty inside too
She's my mum, she's my mum, who cares what other people think
because she's my mum
My mum opened the world to me 'cause she's my mum
She has the best personality
My beautiful mum is so clever
She's the only mum I've got in the world
My mum has the rosiest cheeks in the world.

Kirk Wootten (9)
Henbury Court Primary School

MY MUM

My lovely, lovely mum likes red
She's got a red bedroom
My mum is very nice
She has got a lovely face, blue eyes and lovely beautiful hair
She's nice to me and I am nice to her
She's buys me lovely things that I want for Christmas
I am good for her
She makes me dinner every day
I love her.

Richard Still (9)
Henbury Court Primary School

I AM A WINDOW

I am a window
Leaves bang against me
Children throw stones at me
I see people coming towards me
I feel happy
They knock
They leave me
A traveller comes towards me
He knocks, he calls out
The traveller leaves
I am lonely again.

Matthew Clements (10)
Henbury Court Primary School

MY MUM

My mum is quite fat
She's very, very nice
She's never mean to me
Her hair is brown and straight
Her eyes are brown too
She never ever forgets things
My mum cooks very nice food
My mum is cuddly
My mum is very beautiful
My mum is amazing.

Hannah Mossman (8)
Henbury Court Primary School

DOWN IN THE HALL

I'm all alone huddled tight in my bed,
I need a drink or a snack instead,
I scramble to my feet
As I creep to the door,
My feet start to shiver,
So I fall to the floor.
I stumble back up
Without making a sound,
And I creep to the door
As I walk on the ground.
I sneak down the stairs,
But down in the corner a figure glares.
I tiptoe to the kitchen,
Not knowing at all
That somebody's lurking right down in the hall.

Lucy Martin (9)
Henbury Court Primary School

I AM A WINDOW

I see trees moving in the wind
I see people coming towards me
They had fire on their hands
They tried to burn me
But a man saved me
I was not lonely anymore.

Fatjoni Skonja (9)
Henbury Court Primary School

I Am A Window

I'm an old window
I live in a derelict house
Part of me is cracked
I have big scratches over me
You wouldn't believe it
I'm always alone
Apart from nasty boys who throw stones at me
I see the same things every day
Same old path, same old trees
Same old sunny or gloomy, dark days
Oh, I hate my life.

Jake Still (11)
Henbury Court Primary School

I Am A Window

I am a window
I see trees
The wind comes
It always waves at me
I am so lonely
I am dull and rusty
I see the traveller coming towards me
I shake myself with fear
He leaves
I am so lonely again.

Louise Banfield (9)
Henbury Court Primary School

A LEAF JOURNEY

Today a little autumn journey
He only tells close family,
Because he will meet some on the way
And find them at the end.

First he goes through the snow
He wished he hadn't been born,
But he carries on as snow
Turns to icy rain.

The rain drops on him
Making ice on both sides of him.
He falls heavily, the ice makes it worse,
But saved by some family, setting off.

He sets off to carry on
As he swirls around,
He's near the end, 3, 2, 1,
And he makes it to the bottom.

All his family had died
He flies around, no family alive,
He flies on more but cannot stop
And drowns in the pond.

Andrew Forde (10)
Henbury Court Primary School

RED IS THE COLOUR

Red is the colour of danger
with a horrible stranger.

Red is the colour of my bin
when I tip something in.

Red is the colour of my thumb
when I bang a drum.

Red is the colour of my face
when I have a sweaty race.

Samantha Ford (11)
Henbury Court Primary School

DRAGON SLAYER

He hunts down dragons,
So brave, so bold,
And finds their beds,
Of glimmering gold.
His glistening sword,
Drives through their skin,
Ending their life,
Of deadly sin.

He has his armour,
For dragon's flame,
And has his courage,
For beautiful dame.
His hair is dark,
He's full of might,
So bully him,
He'll want to fight.

So when you're low,
Feeling dim,
Or feeling scared,
Remember him!

George Bowerman (10)
Henbury Court Primary School

WHAT COULD IT BE?

It slithers around
With its green
glaring eyes,
Its bloodthirsty mouth
is drying up.
Angry, waiting,
who could it be?
Who could it be?
It lies waiting for its prey.
Some folks say it's a dragon, maybe,
others may say a ghost.
But who could it be?
What could it be?
Nobody knows.
Nobody knows!

Jade Khan (10)
Henbury Court Primary School

I AM AN OLD WINDOW

I am an old window
Nobody comes to open me
I feel lonely
My handles are getting rusty
I see trees and the moon
The leaves flutter
All the people have gone.

Jamie Morris (9)
Henbury Court Primary School

THE UNICORN

I sit in wonder once again
What is that animal?
With fur as soft as silk
With eyes bright
Shining like stars at night
I ask myself again
What is that animal?
With flowing tail
Sparkling
With a horn changing
Colour as I speak
The unicorn, the unicorn
You hear me say
As I softly gallop away.

Jessica Woods (10)
Henbury Court Primary School

I AM A WINDOW

I am the little window
The moonlight shines on me every night
I see the trees shining at me
Glistening in the starlight
I see the phantoms stare at me
I feel lonely
My hinges are rusty and dirty
I am alone.

Lacey McLeod (9)
Henbury Court Primary School

THE WINDOW

I am a window
I feel lonely and sad
I see trees and leaves
I hear leaves rustling in the wind
I see people walking past taking no notice
The traveller knocks on the door
I feel happy
The traveller leaves
I feel upset and hurt
I am broken
If only people had taken care of me.

Corey Vigne (9)
Henbury Court Primary School

THE LISTENERS

I am an old window
I feel lonely
Nobody comes to open me
Nobody cleans me
I heard a swarm of bees
I see a bunch of flowers
A clump of trees
Every season goes by
I am alone.

Shiny Kim (11)
Henbury Court Primary School

NIGHT

Night is not a peaceful time,
There is horror and much crime,
Spirits creep and shadows leap,
Across the wooden floor,
Waking up in a sweat,
Praying it was just your head,
Owl hooting horror,
'Help! Help! Help!' Children shout.

Night is a giant,
Soaring through the air,
Leaping through the window,
Night is everyone's foe,
Darkness spreading the Earth,
Like a blanket on the bed.

Kelly Ramage (11)
Henbury Court Primary School

I AM A WINDOW

I am an old window
I am always alone
One stormy night along came a man on his horse
Banging on the door as the horse chomps the grass
I am always getting stones thrown at me
Bushes growing all over me
I am just an old window.

Karl Edwards (10)
Henbury Court Primary School

WALK WITH NATURE

On the walk up the Blaise,
A beautiful river lays,
Flowing softly all day.
Dogs and frogs jumping over logs will play.
Children playing happily, cyclists go over bridges carefully.
Squirrels running up a tree,
As the wind blows gracefully.
In the night if you are quiet, you might see a fox or badger.
All through summer,
The sun shines on a flower.
Through the day and through the night,
You will see a beautiful sight.
When you walk on the bumpy trail,
You may see a baby snail.
So if you are passing through Blaise,
You will surely be amazed.

Kimberley Porter Jones (11)
Henbury Court Primary School

DOLPHINS

Dolphins, dolphins
Are so sweet
I think they are really neat.
As I swim across the bay
When it's summer, it is May.
I really wish upon this day
I could meet a dolphin someday.
Then I see my one true wish
To see that beautiful dolphin fish.

Claire Meehan (11)
Henbury Court Primary School

WHAT IS GREEN?

Green is the colour . . . of a fun
Train to play on.

Green is the colour . . . of envy
Green is the colour . . . of beautiful
Grass.

Green is the colour . . . of Mrs Street's
Beautiful eyes.

Green is the colour . . . of wonderful
Leaves in the summer.

Green is the colour . . . of my
Toothbrush belonging to me.

Hannah Verdon (9)
Henbury Court Primary School

THE CALLING OF A CHILD

When I lie in bed at night,
I hear a child crying.
So poor and lonely she is,
You can hear her feet
Pattering on the ground.
You can hear her cry 100 miles away.
Then there's a scream
And a shadow appears
In my old, gloomy bedroom.

Alex Rolfe (9)
Henbury Court Primary School

WHAT IS RED?

Strawberry jam for my tea
Cherry pop for you and me.

Red is the varnish on my toes
In the garden is a prickly rose.

Tomato ketchup on my chips
Red lipstick on my lips.

Red is the Valentine heart
Red raspberries in a jam tart.

Red spots for my chickenpox
I put a letter in the postbox.

Red is the colour of a juicy plum
A fast red car for my mum.

Shannon Tingle (10)
Henbury Court Primary School

I AM ALONE

As I walk beneath the moonlit sky,
I feel so alone and ask myself why.

My wife has left and is far away,
My mournful children emigrated in dismay.

For three years I've been alone,
But why?
I walk beneath the moonlit sky.

I am alone, I know why.

Sarah E Hollier (11)
Henbury Court Primary School

WHAT IS BLUE?

Blue is the whale that splashes over me
Blue is the nice, shiny and sparkly sea.

Blue is the colour of the swimming pool
Blue is the colour that makes me feel cool.

Blue is on my face when I feel sad
Blue is on my face for being so bad.

Blue is the colour of the summer sky
Where the bird flies so high.

Blue is the colour of the bluebell
Which I really love to smell.

Tanya Hughes (10)
Henbury Court Primary School

WHAT IS RED?

Red is the colour of an Arsenal top,
A traffic light saying stop.

Red is the colour of Mars in space,
Red is the colour of an angry face.

Red is the colour of danger,
Never go anywhere with a stranger.

Red is the colour of a sunset in the night,
Red warns us to stop at a traffic light.

Liam Wall (9)
Henbury Court Primary School

THE WEIR

The power of the water
Is crashing and gushing,
Hitting the banks violently,
Flooding the crop-filled land.
Consuming ravenously
All in its path,
Swallowing the fields,
Destroying habitat.
The incredible sight,
The people watch,
Disregarding the dangers
Of the mighty powers.
And the rain continues to fall.

Gary Turner (10)
Henbury Court Primary School

WHAT IS RED?

Red is the colour of a rose,
You might get cut if you get too close.

Red is the colour of a Man U shirt,
Scoring goals, getting hurt.

Red is the colour of traffic lights saying stop,
My angry face that shows I'm hot.

Red is the colour of a Bristol City top,
Like the cherries in the shop.

Damien Elliott (9)
Henbury Court Primary School

SLAY PREY

How may I devour
How may I slay
I may, I may eat my prey
The skin is a reward
But how I kill is a hidden skill
My claws go in
I rip the flesh
I will eat this flesh with my pride
My only pride will be my pride.

Luke Mann & Matthew Hale (11)
Henbury Court Primary School

THE SNAKE

Slithering through the Savanna,
The dry grass brushes scaly skin.
His dark, black tongue flickers out and in,
Once a month he changes his clothes,
He knows exactly where he goes.
He slithers up slowly to his prey,
Then it's that animal's very last day.

Sarah Gray (9)
Henbury Court Primary School

RED

Red is the colour of a flashy sports car.
Red is the raspberries in a jam jar.

Red is the colour of Man United's top.
Red is the sign when I have to stop.

Red is the blood flowing through your heart.
Red is the colour of a dart.

Red is the colour of a lovely rose.
Red is the colour of ribbons and bows.

Red is the colour of a school pen.
'Red is my favourite colour' says Ben.

Red is the ruby in a ring.
Red is the colour of the apples I bring.

Red is the colour of wine.
Red is the jumper I like to be mine.

Red is the colour of cherries.
Red is the colour of berries.

Shane Blake, Ryan Dowden, Carla Gilvear,
Ben, Jodie, Rab & Michelle
Henbury Court Primary School

RED

Red is the colour of Liverpool's top
Like the sign when we have to stop

Red is the colour of the Man Utd shirt
Scoring goals and getting hurt

Red is the colour of my history book
Come inside and have a look

Red is the colour of the sunset
When I'm older I will have a pet

Red is the colour of a postbox
When I'm older I will have spots

Red is the colour of my pencil case
Like some planets in space.

Sammy Rees (9)
Henbury Court Primary School

THEY RISE

As their hands,
Rise from the ground,
The feel of terror,
Is then found,
By the people
Of the town,
Dressed in slippers
And a gown.

As their feet
Come through a hole,
Their faces dark,
As dark as coal,
Now they stand
With arms out wide,
When all the town
Go and hide.

So there . . .
Now you know . . .
I suppose . . .
You'd better *go!*

Fraser Chandler-Jones (11)
Henbury Court Primary School

TORNADO

Sat alone, then all of a sudden it comes . . .
The tornado, it swallows the houses like a greedy tiger.
People run, they run so fast they're like cheetahs on an open plain.
I was scared, I ran and left my belongings behind.
Then it was all over, all the terror for nothing.
The houses that were swallowed, the people that got left behind.
That's what happened when the tornado came.

Jade Hancock (9)
Henbury Court Primary School

CHESIL BEACH

As the waves crash on the rocks, they smash
The sparkling foam spreads over the rippling pebbles
Water is bursting into any gap and spreading into any crack
The sun's reflection sparkles and glistens
Seagulls bobbing up and down on the sparkling sea
It all makes me feel relaxed and free.

Emily Martin (9)
Henbury Court Primary School

DOLPHINS

Dolphins live in the sea
Dolphins are lovely as can be
Dolphins are grey but they may look blue
They stare at me and they stare at you
Dolphins sway, dolphins swing
Hear them whistle, hear them sing.

Jo-Ann Scorrer (10)
Henbury Court Primary School

DEMONS

The consternation ran through me like a bolt,
The blood-curdling demon lopes.
Commanding the deadly underworld,
Like a meercat on patrol.
Guarding the entrance with flames.
His grinding teeth and vicious jaws.
His prey has not a chance.

Michael Harris (11)
Henbury Court Primary School

WHAT IS YELLOW?

Yellow is the . . . lion looking for prey.
Yellow is the . . . sun shining all day.
Yellow is the . . . banana I like to eat.
Yellow is the . . . flame that gives us heat.
Yellow is the . . . sandy beach.
Yellow is the . . . juicy peach.

Shane Mereweather (10)
Henbury Court Primary School

I Am!

I am a simple scrap of paper
Let me be an aeroplane.

I am a fallen leaf
Make me part of a tall tree.

I am a little boy
Help me be a brave knight.

I am a scruffy picture
Make me an embroidered quilt.

Why am I all of these things?
I am!

Sarah Simmonds (10)
Holy Family School

It's A ...

A sun bather
A high jumper
A danger listener
A big footer
A smooth bouncer
A constant chewer
A free explorer
A baby carrier
A loving creature
A fine boxer
It's a . . .
    kangaroo.

Hannah Barry (11)
Holy Family School

WEATHER

I am a gentle breeze,
Make me into a strong tornado.

I am a river,
Make me into the crashing seas.

I am a raindrop,
Make me into a thump of thunder.

I am the gentle sun,
Make me into a forceful storm.

Ross Williams (10)
Holy Family School

I'M ...

A four wheeled
A two pedalled
A wooden framed
A highly strung
A long hinged
A high sounding
A low sounding
A soft, loud
An ivory keyed

I'm a . . . *piano.*

Andrew Collins (10)
Holy Family School

PEACE

I am a symbol of war,
May there be peace.

I am in poverty,
Make me rich.

I am in pain,
Release me.

I am frightened,
Secure me.

I am a National Trust,
I want to grow.

I am at war,
I want to be at home with my family.

I have lost my family,
I want them back.

I am a symbol of war,
May there be peace.

Charlotte Gaffey (11)
Holy Family School

MY POEM

I am a little hamster,
Make me into a roaring tiger.

I am a piece of glass,
Make me a pair of lenses.

I am a scruffy cat,
Make me into a fluffy dog.

I am a drop of rain,
Make me a part of the ocean.

Rebecca Arthur (11)
Holy Family School

A SIMPLE SCRAP OF PAPER

I am a simple scrap of paper,
Give me wings so that I can fly.

I am an old, rusty bike,
Transform me into a fashionable vehicle.

I am a bare tree in a deserted field,
Give me leaves and make me beautiful once more.

I am a torn chair in a cold, dark room,
Repair me so someone famous can sit on me once more.

I am a simple scrap of paper,
Please give me another chance in life.

Jessica Hogan (10)
Holy Family School

I AM A SIMPLE SCRAP OF PAPER

I am a simple scrap of paper,
Make me an aeroplane that soars through the clouds.

I am a lifeless rubber,
Send me back to my home, the forest.

I am a dirty, worn out, banger of a car,
My ambition is to be a luxurious BMW.

I am a piece of broken glass,
Make me part of the Queen's palace window.

I am a poor, homeless child,
Please may I have a family so I can have some love
and warmth once again.

I am an unfortunate, unused stone,
Mould me back into my mother, the mountain.

I am a bent paper clip,
I would really like it if I was to become a £2 coin.

I am an old, used, plain pen,
Make me a fine fountain pen that will assist somebody special.

I am a worthless, empty ink cartridge,
Refill me and I will happily help the pen to write the children's
brilliant stories and poems.

I am a rusty staple,
I beg you to make me worth something again.

I am a weak, wounded mouse,
I would really appreciate it if you made me healthy
so I could run once again.

I am a simple piece of scrap paper,
Make me anything but what I am.

Jacob Scott (10)
Holy Family School

I AM . . .

I am a simple scrap of paper
Take me back to the forest where I belong.

I am a blunt pencil
Make me nice and sharp.

I am a torn-apart teddy bear
Bring me to those gentle arms.

I am a beadless rattle
Give me some beads so I can vibrate.

I am a baby crying for my mum
Call my mum so I can giggle.

I am a puppy all alone
Find me an owner so I can be stroked.

Tara Keary (10)
Holy Family School

WHAT IS IT?

It's . . .

A great eater
A sea creeper
A deep sea diver
A fantastic hider
A fish eater
A tail swisher
A joyful player
A great flyer
A water groover
A great friend.

(It's a dolphin!)

Laura Bradford (10)
Holy Family School

I AM A YOUNG BOY CALLED ROB

I am a young boy called Rob,
My mum says I'm such a slob,
She got me a broom,
And said 'Tidy your room,
And make sure you do a good job.'

Larry West (11)
Holy Family School

I'M HUNGRY

'I'm hungry Mum'
'Wait till tea.'

'Can I have this ice lolly please?'
'No, wait till tea.'

'Can I have a bag of crisps?'
'No, wait till tea.'

'Can I have a chocolate bar?'
'No, wait till tea!'

'Tea's ready!'
'Mum, I'm not hungry . . . '

Daniel Roper (11)
Holy Family School

IT'S A . . .

A fast mover
A water groover
A fish hoover
A large monster
A day sleeper
A fish order
A sea diver
A bay stalker
A grey nurser
A sharp-toothed gnasher.

Shark!

Sam Lawfull (10)
Holy Family School

CONSTANTINE BAY

As I walked across the golden, sandy beach,
with the waves lapping at my feet,
shafts of sunlight sparkling like open jaws
on the razor-sharp rocks.
Crabs pinching like killing blades at my toes
and bobbing boats as their deep, dark shadows
swaying on the surface.

Children screaming with delight
as they dart across the hot, burning
North Cornwall sand dunes.
As the sun sets I stop, I think, how does the sea and its
family live their lives and survive?

Keelan Hole (10)
Oldbury-on-Severn Primary School

THE MELTING SUN

The golden treacle sun disappears behind the
dark, shadowy hills.
The red fiery sky turns into the dark, blue
sky.
Then the moon shoots into the sky,
like a shooting star, filling the sky with
moonlight and stars.
The stars sparkle like a disco ball and the
moonlight twinkles down on our
small, little planet.

Alice Porter (9)
Oldbury-on-Severn Primary School

NATURE'S 'BLOWING IN THE WIND'

The shimmering sun hits the water like a bullet
as it glistens like a coral reef.
Lapping waves eat the bank
as ripples run wild and free.

The plain of grass looks like a desert of daisies
swaying in the breeze.
The huge rainbow mountains shine
with their shadows covering the desert of grass.

Old, rotten logs bob up and down.
Spears of sunlight dance over the river,
then slowly the sun sets.

Jessica Young (10)
Oldbury-on-Severn Primary School

A GANGSTER IS . . .

A gangster is as painful as an open wound.
As cunning as a sly fox.
He's always alert and on guard.
As hurtful as a dagger with a jagged edge.
As strong as an ox.
His nifty ability to shoot and run is twinned
            to an inflamed paper cut.
He's as sharp as a blade.
As dark as the night sky.
As white as a corpse.
He is as nasty as a grazed knee.
He's like a pack of wild wolves.

Benjamin Pearce (11)
Oldbury-on-Severn Primary School

ROLLING DOWN THE MOUNTAIN

The wind rolled down the mountain tops
and across the golden sand dunes,
sweeping up the sand.
Whispering wind blows against me
as clouds of sea spray dances around me,
swirling and twirling.
Sandy water delivers puddles on the beach.
Seaweed is turning, whirling into a hurricane.
The heat of the silver moonlight warms my face
and the stars twinkle beside me.
I dig my feet into the sand
and feel it between my toes.

Ashley Stott (11)
Oldbury-on-Severn Primary School

DAD

He is Chelsea blue
On a hot summer's day on a footie pitch.
Gran Canaria on the beach
And a hot ray of sun.
A Winterbourne footie kit.
A leather settee.
Dream Team man
And a chef's seafood special.

Tom May (10)
Oldbury-on-Severn Primary School

THE DECAYING OAK

The mass of twisted branches stood motionless
as the whispering chill echoed through the bare, lonely field.
The branches stretched out.
The crooked figure bent down as if the mass was ashamed.

The chipped bark scarred the crooked figure.
The mass's grave was dirty, dusty
and the figure wasted away in silence.

The foggy memories of youth were joyful and happy.
The young tree shot its way up, weaving towards the clouds above,
but one more stab in the back
and the great mass collapsed into its bare, lonely grave.

Emma Palmer (10)
Oldbury-on-Severn Primary School

SUNLIGHT

Sunlight is beaming down on the church roof
With daffodils sat outside like 1000 yellow bugles.

The clouds are white
And look like paint on a blue canvas.

The smell of fresh-cut grass
Is drifting through the air like a hot air balloon.

The old stone path winds round
Leading to a gloomy graveyard.

Chantelle Rugman (11)
Oldbury-on-Severn Primary School

THE BLACK AND WHITE THEATRE

The black and white theatre
It's full of darkness and black.
It's an area where time has stopped
It's so cold, it's like Pluto.
You can hear the footsteps of the moving stars.
As I step out into the colourful city
I look back at the black and white theatre.

Alex Ujvarosy (9)
Oldbury-on-Severn Primary School

THE HIDDEN TREASURE

There was once a dog who was going for a walk,
Then he heard a parrot talk.
'Come with me today. Stand and watch
the children play.
Follow me and I will lead you away.
I will take you into hidden caves,
Where people jump over big waves.
In the cave there is a chest,
Where people outside play and say hooray!
No one here can lift the lid,
But I can, I can.
If you will help me open the chest,
You can have a rest.
When we see the treasure shine,
It will be mine!'

Sally Page (9)
Rangeworthy CE Primary School

HIDDEN TREASURE

There was a man from Leicester,
Who always went searching for treasure.
He fell down a hole,
And met a mole,
And said, 'Hello! I'm Sylvester!'

The mole had a brilliant headlight,
Because he didn't have very good eyesight.
He stepped on a bug,
It crunched and he dug,
And he disappeared out of sight.

'I'm all on my own!' cried Sylvester.
'I wish I was back in Leicester!
I've forgotten my map,
I want to go back,
Now I'll never find any treasure!'

'Wait a second!' Sylvester cried.
'I've finally found some treasure,' he sighed.
'I would have searched,
From my birth
For this till the day I died!'

'I'll go and get some help,' Sylvester said.
'I'll go and get the local med.
I think I've broke
My leg, I'll choke
If I don't get some treatment, then bed!'

As for the treasure, 'Yipee!' he did cry.
'I'll look after this until the day I die!'

Andrew Hewitt (10)
Rangeworthy CE Primary School

HIDDEN TREASURE

There is a place in the middle of the sea
It is just for you and me.
We have got a chance of getting the treasure
If you get the right measure.
We have got to cross a lake
We will get the treasure if we don't make a mistake.
The treasure is buried in the ground
But there might be traps, so don't make a sound.
Run to the boat
Look there's a note
Floating in the sea.
You can open it, no you not me.
So they both picked up the note
And put it in their boat.
They sailed off back home
All the way to Rome.

Francinne Gigg (10)
Rangeworthy CE Primary School

HIDDEN TREASURE

Two girls were walking on the beach,
One girl was eating a peach.
They found a map
And put on their caps.

They went to see
And found a flea,
At the bottom of the shore,
Next to a big, black door.

They found the cross,
Which was covered in moss,
With a big, white shark on top.
He nearly popped!

Rosie Hale (9)
Rangeworthy CE Primary School

HIDDEN TREASURES

There was a bloodthirsty pirate,
Who in danger decided to migrate.
Whilst on his way,
He tried not to pay,
The people he owed who were irate.

'I don't have any money,' the pirate said,
'So let's put this problem to bed.
I know about some treasure,
Which will bring you great pleasure,
Don't you think you could have that instead?'

After the pirate fell in a hole,
And saw a gigantic, humungous big mole.
He drew patterns in the ground,
Around and around,
Then whacked his big head on a pole!

'It's a mad mole,' the pirate said,
'I must be dreaming in my bed.'
Just then there was a golden gleam,
In a distant, muddy, murky stream.
'*Yahoo!* It's the treasure, it's not lead,
But I wish I'd stop hitting my head!'

Alex Smith (11)
Rangeworthy CE Primary School

HIDDEN TREASURE

Hidden treasure under the sea
Is waiting for me
Down, down, the treasure lurks
Down, if I find it I will have lots of perks
Extraordinary sights I will see
Now I can see tonnes and tonnes of treasure
Rocks and rubble beneath the surface
Everyone is trying to find it
As sure as shore
Shivering by the water
Under the rocks creepy-crawlies play
Restraining intruders as they come
Everlasting treasure hidden.

Nicholas Bird (11)
Rangeworthy CE Primary School

HIDDEN TREASURE

Down in the sea where nobody knows
the hidden treasure is under a stone.
Still looking is Captain Crook,
if it's not found soon he'll continue to moan.

Captain Crook soon found a map,
all his mates wanted to go there.
Soon after he found a pole
with a sign saying 'that way!'
They found a chest and opened it up
but it was bare.

Kirsty Harding (9)
Rangeworthy CE Primary School

HIDDEN TREASURE

Deep, deep under the sea,
There was a box of treasure for us to see,
Full of goodies we don't know.
If you want to know where the treasure is,
Follow the boat with a big yellow strip.
Mind the shark with its sharp teeth,
And on your journey you'll have to find the key.
The key is big, bright and bold with a gold cap.
Follow and you will find the treasure
Under the sandy vine.
Open the chest and you will find
Jewellery and gold and presents that you desire.

Bethany Morgan (11)
Rangeworthy CE Primary School

A FROSTY POEM

As we gallop through
the crunchy, frostbitten grass,
I stare at the thick blanket of steam
billowing from the castle of frost.
We scream and shout
as we pass the brilliant white trees.
Stomping feet crackle,
crunching dry leaves to dust.
The freezing cold snow
froze our toes to ice.

James Steer (9)
Raysfield Junior School

A COLD CHRISTMAS

Golden brown twigs covered in frost.
Sparkling yellow leaves drifting to the ground.
Twinkling ice covers the shimmering grass
so none can be found.

The icy wind rushes through my fingertips.
Feathery icicles sprouting off frozen leaves.
The crystal clear sky like Sprite,
refreshing and bright.

Frosty, wet trees dripping evaporated snow
to the floor.
The bright shining sun shone through
the misty sky.
Crunchy steps underfoot,
while walking along a snowy path.

Bradley Arkwright (10)
Raysfield Junior School

VALENTINE'S DAY

All over the street,
Love is in the air,
Roses and chocolate everywhere.
Decorations for romantic days,
Lots of hugs and kisses,
Love is precious in your heart.
The sun is setting on the hill,
That is what you call
Romantic.

Amy Norcombe (9) & Jade Ball (10)
Raysfield Junior School

FROSTY

One frosty day,
It was icy like an iceberg,
Feathery-like snowy leaves,
Glittery, shiny logs,
Gleaming white frost and snow,
Crunchy grass when you walk,
Crystal clear sky,
Golden brown shiny trees,
Sparkly crystal shoes,
And sugary yellow sun.
Then I walked along more and saw,
Long, green grass with sugary ice on,
Grey smoke coming off the wooden castle,
Emerald green grass turning into frost,
And a lovely red-belly robin sitting on
the roof of a school.

Louise Down (9)
Raysfield Junior School

A ROMANTIC DAY

On Valentine's Day
You will get all the love
You want,
Chocolate
And cards,
And I'm sure
Much more.

Emma Pitman & Kirsty McNeill (9)
Raysfield Junior School

TWILIGHT MYSTERIES

The black night sky all so pitch-black.
Nothing could be seen
But white dots glowing in twilight skies.
The creeping twilight cat
Pouncing through the night skies.

The night-time skies
So mysteriously black.
The trees all still and asleep.
The ponds also still.
Not a movement.

The mysteries of night are great.
At night-time little mice scurry.
Creeping cats pounce.
Floating glow-worms in the sky.
A very dark and still sight.

As soon as night sprouts away daylight,
Everything's a complete standstill.
Everything warmly wrapped up
As dark moonlight strikes.

Stuart Russell (9)
Raysfield Junior School

MYSTIC MAGIC

Higglety, pigglty, bing, bang, bong!
Iggly, oggly, iggly, hogglc, wigg!
Ibblenignog, obble, scwogle!
Yubble, dubble, gong, dong, don!

Mooeydooey, hongongphooey!
Kibble, kobble, nibble, nobble!
Dingdong, noddlepoddle, nobb!
Mystic magic do your stuff!

Sammy Wilsmore (10) & Andrea Berry (9)
Raysfield Junior School

THE SPACE RACE

Aliens from everywhere,
They want to come and race,
You'd better hurry up,
Or they will even take your place.

The spaceships are different colours,
Some of them are blue.
They are ready at the starting line,
They know what to do.

They're flying through the dark blue sky,
The spaceships are very fast.
They're gliding round the stars and moon,
And one of them will be last.

The moon is a big white crescent,
And the stars are shiny and yellow.
The Earth is like a big green football,
And the sky is like a massive blue meadow.

One of the aliens has won the cup,
Because he fired lasers out of the window.
One of the aliens was last in the race,
Because he was so slow!

Matthew Lawes (8)
Redfield Edge Primary School

THE HUNGRY JELLYFISH

Once there was a jellyfish,
Who wanted some jelly,
But didn't have a jelly dish.
   Empty belly!
So he went to get some rice,
The shop had been invaded by mice.
   Empty belly!
So he went to get some chips,
From fishy snack bar,
They didn't have any dips,
Only jelly in a jar,
He ate it.
   Full belly!
He needed a drink,
But he couldn't think,
Juice or pop,
   So he had the lot!

Edward Searle (8)
Redfield Edge Primary School

THE BUBBLE

It goes so high
It is so fat
It is so shiny
It pops on a lap
What is it?
A bubble.

Matthew Ollis (8)
Redfield Edge Primary School

THE SUN AND THE RAIN

The sun is shining,
The rain is whining.
People are playing,
People are saying,
'Time to play,
Hip, hip, hooray!'
A game inside,
No outside ride.
The paddling pool out,
Going out and about.
No playtime now,
Just an inside row.

Laura Bennett (8)
Redfield Edge Primary School

MY LITTLE BROTHER

My little brother
Is really weird.
His name is Ben
And he has no fears.
I call him 'big face'
My mum and dad
Call him 'big ears'.

Paige Gilbert (8)
Redfield Edge Primary School

CLOWNS

Once I saw a clown
When I went to the fair.
He had a red hat
And chestnut hair.
He wore a bright red nose
And very colourful clothes.
He ran round and round in the Big Top,
Chasing all the other clowns,
Spraying water in their faces
And throwing custard pies.
But he was so funny,
He brought tears to my eyes.

Kaisha Thatcher (8)
Redfield Edge Primary School

KITTENS

Small and fluffy,
Fit in your hand,
Sleep in your bed
And play in the sand.
Jump all over,
Play with mice,
Run around
Being sweet and nice.

Aiysha Bishop (8)
Redfield Edge Primary School

WINGS

If I had wings I would gaze at the sunset
and touch the fluffy clouds.
If I had wings I would fly around the rainbow
and sing with the birds.
If I had wings I would swim with the sea
across the ocean.

Katie Edgell (8)
Redfield Edge Primary School

UNTITLED

A food lover
A rhythmic walker
A stylish jumper
A quick canter
A loyal friend!

Sam Jones (8)
Saltford Primary School

FIRST DAY BACK

First day back
What a shock
Everybody looks good
I've just got a frock.

Alice Mould (8)
Saltford Primary School

HIDDEN TREASURES

There was a mouse
Who lived in a house.
There was a cat
Who sat on a mat.
There was a dog
Who lay on a log.
There was a bird
Who always came third.
There was a fish
Who crouched in a dish.
There was a bunny
Who guarded money.
There was a pig
Who wore a wig.
There was a hare
Who jumped on a chair.
Then there's me
Who's watching TV.

Naomi Pattinson
Saltford Primary School

HIDDEN TREASURES

I hope I find a treasure today, like yesterday.
I hope I find a treasure today, to hold me warm and snug.
I hope I find a treasure today that makes me laugh a lot.
I hope I find a treasure today that helps me learn to write.
I found a treasure today and it was love.

Eleanor Hogg (8)
Saltford Primary School

HIDDEN TREASURES

I'm dreaming about some hidden treasure
Looking for it is such fun
I'm with a man who is a pleasure
And gives me lots of buns.

We looked around the USA
But all we found was rocks
So we went back to England, hey
But all we found was a fox.

Suddenly I'm back at home
And at the side of my bed there's a box
So I open it up and find a comb
And a big, brown fox.

Sarah-Jane May (9)
Saltford Primary School

HIDDEN TREASURE

A girl has gone to an island
As far away as Thailand.
She's looking for the treasure
It's not much of a leisure.

Then she saw a sparkle
Next she saw some charcoal.
All around a chest
It was simply the best.

Katherine O'Hanlon (8)
Saltford Primary School

HIDDEN TREASURES

We're on a secret mission
To try to find the treasure
This is not non-fiction
It's all our secret leisure

Where can it be?
This is so annoying
Do I need a key?
Or shall I do some sawing?

We're on a secret mission
To try and find some treasure
This is not non-fiction
It's all our secret leisure
Good luck!

Rosie Stonehouse (8)
Saltford Primary School

PUDDLES

Splashing around
in a big blue thing,
while rain is trickling down.
A splash here
and a splash there
and a splash
everywhere!

Lucy Boulton (8)
Saltford Primary School

HIDDEN TREASURE

Think of spring,
With birds singing.
Think of summer,
Liked by a runner.
Think of winter,
Good for a sledger.
Think of autumn,
And God who brought them.

Jonty Taylor (8)
Saltford Primary School

GUESS WHO?

Good swimmer
Dog winner

Best hugger
Rope tugger

Face licker
Shoe nicker.

My dog Bertie.

Hannah Charles (8)
Saltford Primary School

TIGERS

Tigers black, tigers orange
Tigers' forest everywhere
Tigers play, tigers' day,
Tigers cute and cuddly.

Ben Clarke (9)
Saltford Primary School

HIDDEN TREASURE

I want to find some pirate treasure,
In this house or not,
I've got my pirate hat,
I'm sailing in my cardboard boat,
Here with my telescope.

Now I've found a map,
Here's an arrow,
This way,
Here I must dig,
Wow, the treasure is a pirate lunch.

Philippa Parfrey (8)
Saltford Primary School

GUESS WHO?

Animal lover
She loves her mother

Medium runner
She's a lot funner

She likes swimming
And she also likes singing

Me!

Hannah Bailey (8)
Saltford Primary School

TIGERS

Tigers orange
Tigers black
Tigers everywhere
Tigers attack.

Daniel Haycocks (9)
Saltford Primary School

AUTUMN POEM

When the autumn comes
The golden apples look like red, shiny balls.
The leaves look like beautiful rainbows.
The trees go bare like a piece of grass.
The chestnuts get roasted like chicken
Because when it's autumn, it's fun.
Fun like anything.

When the robin comes,
The squirrels curl up like children in their beds.
The leaves fall like helpless feathers.
The children collect sycamore seeds like squirrels
                                   with nuts.
Because it's autumn, it's fun.
Fun like anything.

Jennifer Roake (8)
Westbury on Trym CE Primary School

AUTUMN POEM

When it is autumn,
We see roots under soil like witches' fingers,
We hear brown leaves crunch like chocolate munch,
We smell chestnuts cook like a blaze of fire,
We go for walks in the wood like running around,
Because when it is autumn things change,
Things change when it is autumn.

When it is fireworks night,
We see fireworks glistening like gems in night light,
We hear fireworks popping like balls dropping,
We smell bonfires burning which twinkle noses,
We go to firework displays that make me scream,
Because things are scary that night,
Things are scary that night.

Maria Neary (7)
Westbury on Trym CE Primary School

AUTUMN POEM

When it's autumn,
The leaves fall like summer butterflies.
The squirrels collect like tigers hunting.
The birds eat food like Romans invading.
The conkers fall like little bombs
Because when it's autumn things change,
Things change when it's autumn.

When it's autumn,
I trick and treat like ghouls running.
I smell roasting chestnuts like bonfires burning.
I dance like a dancing pirate.
I run like guns firing
Because when it's autumn things change,
Things change when it's autumn.

Jade Salmon (8)
Westbury on Trym CE Primary School

AUTUMN POEM

When it's autumn
The pumpkins glow like candles.
The conkers fall like falling birds,
The foxes run like shooting stars.
The dead leaves are like Guy Fawkes,
The birds fly like bombs in the sky
Because when it's autumn things change,
Things change when it's autumn.

When it's autumn
I crunch the leaves in the cold.
I hear bonfires crackling,
I hear fireworks going off in the sky
Because when it's autumn things change,
Things change when it's autumn.

Kelly Sessions (8)
Westbury on Trym CE Primary School